The Cato Institute

The Cato Institute is named for the libertarian pamphlets *Cato's Letters,* which were inspired by the Roman Stoic Cato the Younger. Written by John Trenchard and Thomas Gordon, *Cato's Letters* were widely read in the American colonies in the early eighteenth century and played a major role in laying the philosophical foundation for the revolution that followed.

The erosion of civil and economic liberties in the modern world has occurred in concert with a widening array of social problems. These disturbing developments have resulted from a major failure to examine social problems in terms of the fundamental principles of human dignity, economic welfare, and justice.

The Cato Institute aims to broaden public policy debate by sponsoring programs designed to assist both the scholar and the concerned layperson in analyzing questions of political economy.

The programs of the Cato Institute include the sponsorship and publication of basic research in social philosophy and public policy; publication of major journals on the scholarship of liberty and commentary on political affairs; production of debate forums for radio; and organization of an extensive program of symposia, seminars, and conferences.

CATO INSTITUTE
747 Front Street
San Francisco, California 94111

Revisionism:
A Key to Peace
and Other Essays

Revisionism: A Key to Peace and Other Essays

Harry Elmer Barnes

With a Foreword by James J. Martin

CATO PAPER No. 12

CATO INSTITUTE

San Francisco, California

"Revisionism: A Key to Peace" is reprinted by permission of the copyright holder, Ralph Myles, Publisher, Colorado Springs, Colorado, © 1966.
"Revisionism and the Historical Blackout" is reprinted by permission of the copyright holder, The Caxton Printers, Ltd., Caldwell, Idaho, © 1953.
"How 'Nineteen Eighty-Four' Trends Threaten American Peace, Freedom, and Prosperity" is reprinted by permission of the copyright holder, The Caxton Printers, Ltd., Caldwell, Idaho.

Library of Congress Cataloging in Publication Data

Barnes, Harry Elmer, 1889-1968.
  Revisionism, a key to peace and other essays.

  (Cato paper ; no. 12)
  Bibliography: p.
  CONTENTS: Revisionism, a key to peace.—Revisionism and the historical blackout.—How "Nineteen eighty-four" trends threaten American peace, freedom, and prosperity.
    1. World War, 1939-1945—Historiography—Addresses, essays, lectures. 2. European War, 1914-1918—Historiography—Addresses, essays, lectures. 3. United States—Foreign relations—1945-   —Addresses, essays, lectures. 4. United States—Politics and government—1945-   —Addresses, essays, lectures. I. Title.
D743.42.B37   1980   940.53'072   80-15902
ISBN 0-932790-18-6

Printed in the United States of America

CATO INSTITUTE
747 Front Street
San Francisco, California 94111

CONTENTS

FOREWORD

Of the many forms taken by man's restless curiosity, none is more characteristically human than the endless contemplation of the past. This preoccupation leads to the continual revising of history, which is made necessary not only by the discovery of new or previously suppressed facts but also by new interpretations of the meaning of the past and attempts to see it in the light of the present. In every area where some healthy interest prevails, change is to be expected; as Margaret Mead once observed, a field without new research is a dying field. One might say that revision is the state of affairs in every live department of learning and that the scope of such revision and its speed and influence are the things that distinguish one academic center from another.

The term "revisionism" is used in many quite distinct settings (e.g., Marxist revisionism and Old Testament revisionism), but it is perhaps most familiar when applied to the schools of historical criticism that arose after each world war. It is almost impossible to become even moderately aware of this revisionism without encountering repeatedly the work and influence of Harry Elmer Barnes (1889-1968).*

In the dozen years since his death, HEB's formidable reputation has continued to grow, and his work has often been cited by supporters and critics alike. But his revisionist writings, printed originally in modest quantities (large publishers were far more interested in distributing his general works in the fields of history, sociology, and criminology), have become almost unavailable.

My first acquaintance with Barnes came in the fall of 1938 at

---

*Indispensable to an understanding of the scope of Barnes's intellectual interests and his amazing literary productivity is the symposium edited by Arthur Goddard, *Harry Elmer Barnes, Learned Crusader: The New History in Action* (Colorado Springs: Ralph Myles, 1968).

the University of New Hampshire, where my freshman history textbook was his massive, two thousand–page *History of Western Civilization*. Reading it was an ordeal for all of us students because we didn't have the background to cope with such a compendium of learning. It was seven years before I acquired the knowledge that made possible a profitable reading of the book. Nevertheless, I am unendingly grateful to my instructor, Professor Allan B. Partridge, for assigning it.

My personal contact with Barnes began a decade later when I saw in Frank Chodorov's monthly broadsheet *analysis* a short but kindly review of the first edition of HEB's trenchant brochure *The Struggle Against the Historical Blackout*. It eventually went through nine editions, all self-published, which provided readers the world over with an understanding of the basic issue in the contest between the official establishment account of the just-concluded global war (an account that enjoyed the warm favor and lavish material support of the new world power structure that grew out of the war) and the account being put together so painfully and at great personal cost by a small contingent of critics.

My request for a copy led to a correspondence that continued for twenty years, often at the rate of three letters a week. It was punctuated by many meetings, which took place in New York and California and at several places in between. The earliest of these occurred shortly after Labor Day 1952, when I stopped to see him for a few days at Stonewood, his incredible hillside spread overlooking Lake Otsego, a few miles from Cooperstown, N.Y. It was then that I first saw part of the symposium that was to be published the following year under the title *Perpetual War for Perpetual Peace* (echoing a phrase used by Charles A. Beard), along with galley proof of an equally important revisionist classic, also published in 1953, the English barrister F. J. P. Veale's *Advance to Barbarism*.

"Revisionism and the Historical Blackout," HEB's leadoff chapter in *Perpetual War*, is a restatement of a large part of his earlier *Struggle Against the Historical Blackout*. The publication of *Perpetual War* took place at about the same time that the second volume of the ponderous set of establishment tomes produced by Professors William L. Langer and S. Everett Gleason came out. The reader of 1953 could thus read one against the other, these works ideally representing the two sides of the confrontation between the revisionists and those whom Barnes described as the "blackout boys." (In the controversy between the same representative forces after 1918 concerning the First World War, the contenders were frequently identified as the revisionists and the salvagers, whose job it was to "salvage" as much of the wartime propaganda as possible from the revisionist revelations.)

Few people in the postwar world could appreciate what revisionists were up against in the forces represented by Langer and Gleason. People were too distracted by commonplace political verbiage to understand the consequences of the revolution that had occurred since the summer of 1944, probably best exemplified by the turnaround that found people such as Senator Arthur Vandenberg and John Foster Dulles joining the Roosevelt warrior regime in its preliminary proposals outlining the "postwar world." This political *renversement,* announcing a change of sweeping dimensions and signaling the coming American imperial investment of the world (the "American Century" vision of Henry Luce fleshed out) under the cover of what was to be known as "bipartisan foreign policy" ("politics stops at the water's edge"), took many of us a few more years to grasp.

But the facts were all there on the jacket flaps and in the front matter of Langer and Gleason's two volumes: Bankrolled by a six-figure grant (an immense sum to underwrite a book with thirty years ago) from the Rockefeller millions and proudly announced on the title page as "published for the Council on Foreign Relations" (which even owned the copyright), *The World Crisis and American Foreign Policy* had been frankly described as a deliberate effort to solidify the interventionist and internationalist version of how the United States had become a belligerent in World War II and why the world that followed 1945 was taking the direction it was.

Professor Langer, a formidable figure in Harvard University's history department, was additionally identified as chief of the research and analysis branch of the wartime cloak-and-dagger American intelligence force, the Office of Strategic Services (OSS), which smoothly metamorphosed into the postwar Central Intelligence Agency (CIA), with Langer becoming its first Assistant Director. His partner, Professor Gleason, lately of the Amherst College history department (schools in the Little Ivy League supplied a disproportionately large number of people to the OSS, especially Williams College) had many of the same credentials as Langer. Chief of the intelligence staff of the OSS, Gleason had been the intelligence representative from the OSS to the Joint Chiefs of Staff during the war, and at publication time he was deputy executive secretary of the National Security Council. One must admit these were heady and dramatic jobs compared with the humdrum of pedagogy in what Beard and Thorstein Veblen were wont to describe as "hire" education.

Nothing could have demonstrated better that policy needs proper historical justification than these lavish books by Langer and Gleason, published with the hope that they would head off an attack like the wave of post-1918 revisionist debunking of the war that was supposed to make the world safe for democracy. But it was their fate to run into *Perpetual War* immediately, and instead of encountering uncritical acceptance in the manner of medieval court history, the Langer and Gleason works, and the many supporting volumes from a score of other pedagogues and scribes-turned-warrior, came on the scene only to be met head-on by a succession of harsh and critical studies contradicting them at almost every corner.

Langer and Gleason were not the only protagonists of the new dispensation who traded academic robes for wartime garb and subsequent high rank and opulence in the post-1945 world, which the wartime advertisers with nothing to sell promised us would be the "golden postwar future" (as the sardonic revisionist Professor Fred Shannon once remarked, it turned out to consist of the ballpoint pen). There were among them the likes of Herbert Feis, a State Department functionary during the war, Arthur Schlesinger, Jr., a minor figure in the OSS in France, and the magisterial Samuel Eliot Morison of Harvard, the Walter Cronkite of American History professors, who was elevated to high rank by President Roosevelt himself to prepare an official history of U.S. wartime naval operations and subsequently promoted to admiral. (One can imagine the jeers and corrosive commentary from the American academy on the Japanese professor selected by a victorious Tojo to write the official naval history of the Pacific war.) At one time or another, and repeatedly, Barnes took on all these, and several other, supporters of the official line, but Langer got it worst, in one of Barnes's most arresting *samizdat* booklets, *The Court Historians versus Revisionism* (1952).

Perpetual War for Perpetual Peace, like Barnes's massive labor on World War I, *The Genesis of the World War,* was not a commercial success; it was kept in print less than a third as long and remaindered early in 1959. Most of these copies were donated to libraries, and, where they in fact entered the catalogued holdings (gifts to libraries offensive to liberal sensitivities have a way of finding prompt disposal via the circular file), continued to enhance the authors' reputations and influence. Sustained interest kept demand for the book steady for two decades and led to at least one high-priced reprint. Barnes's chapter in *Perpetual War* elaborating on the bibliography and consequences of revisionist scholarship is probably his best treatment of the subject.

Of a somewhat different nature is his long essay "Revisionism: A Key to Peace," which was featured in the Spring 1966 issue (vol. II, no. 1) of *Rampart Journal,* a short-lived and much lamented libertarian quarterly. This number is unique in that it is the only known issue of a serial publication entirely devoted to World War II revisionist contributions.

Since it went out to less than a thousand subscribers, it is a work of considerably greater scarcity than *Perpetual War.* It is being reprinted here for the first time. In the dozen years that had elapsed since the publication of *Perpetual War*, a substantial list of new works had been added to the revisionist library. But Barnes went far beyond bibliographical criticisms and commentary. He managed to project the entire substance of the revisionist approach in a remarkable condensation of parts of about six earlier labors, including the salient portions of *Blasting the Historical Blackout* and *Revisionism and Brainwashing*, both self-published in 1963. This essay, one of his last four on World War II revisionism, had gone the rounds of a few of us for criticisms and suggestions prior to publication; I considered it a privilege to be a contributor to the issue in which it appeared.

The third essay in this selection of Barnes's revisionist work will be especially welcome to those familiar with his other work who are seeing this essay for the first time. Intended to be the last chapter of *Perpetual War*, and set in corrected galleys since late in 1952, "How 'Nineteen Eighty-Four' Trends Threaten American Peace, Freedom, and Prosperity" is indeed a major addition to revisionist literature. I have had a copy of these galleys in my possession for many years and have mentioned them and allowed them to be examined at many revisionist symposia, most recently in 1974 and 1975.

I discussed the piece with HEB on several occasions but never did learn why the decision was made to set it aside. If one reads carefully, however, it becomes obvious that this forthright libertarian analysis (he even quotes F. A. "Baldy" Harper) gave absolutely no comfort to any conventional political viewpoint at large in the early 1950s.

One may search the literature of the early 1950s from beginning to end and still find nothing as excellent as this resolute assault on the new establishment outlook and its consequences. Barnes has no mercy here on any political faction or party. He assails them all, from the conservatives to the Communists, but especially the new totalitarian-liberal middle, the so-called "vital center" that the recently concluded war had formed by homogenizing all the formerly distinct parts of the probelligerence and interventionist spectrum.

HEB and I corresponded extensively after his famous appearance at a session on World War II at the American Historical Association's meeting in Chicago in December 1950. We mulled over trends in world affairs and how they harmonized, sometimes uncannily, with the prescriptions in George Orwell's now celebrated novel *1984*, which had been published midway in 1949. A further dimension was added to our ruminations by George Lundberg, professor of sociology at the University of Washington in Seattle, a contributor to *Perpetual War* and also a close student of the Orwellian view of the world politics emerging after 1945. (Harry introduced me at social gatherings in the 1950s as his "expert on Orwellian tendencies," but the substance of his work under discussion here involved the observations made in a rather wide round robin of correspondence.)

The remarkable thing is that a very large part of this viewpoint and analysis has held up so well through a generation, and several of the predictions have had an eerie coincidence with actual events. (Who was talking over here about the spread of the war in Asia to Vietnam in *1952*? We were, although mainly as a consequence of noticing the effort of the French to reestablish their dominance there, as they tried to do also in Syria and North Africa. In view of what has been happening in recent years, the basic Orwellian theme, which is *the use of "foreign policy" to control and direct domestic policy* (actually developed in a remarkably similar way by Professor Michael Cochran for H. L. Mencken's *American Mercury* as far back as 1932), as elaborated upon here by Barnes, is probably even more pressing now than it was when he brought this essay together in 1952.

Revisionist penetration of what Harry Elmer Barnes described as the "historical blackout," has occurred, over a period of time, in such a way that perhaps most of it has been unperceived. The global establishment, except that part represented by world communism, has given ground steadily in some areas. It has also managed to incorporate some revisionism into the official record in such a manner that latecomers are incapable of discerning that changes have been made. Admissions of previous ignorance, obfuscation, or mendacity have been made so unobtrusively that one would never know that there are facts and arguments quite at variance with what is now put forward. On some matters, nevertheless, the original establishment line remains unaltered, and the mass media, particularly television, continue with almost eerie aplomb to put forward an account of the coming of the war, how it was fought, and its consequences that coincides with the original interventionist propaganda. From television presentations, one would never suspect a line had been written challenging this often unbelievably innocent and simplemindedly superficial narrative.

World War I revisionism had a public phase in which popular accounts written with great skill and appeal made remarkable impact upon the opinions of the general run of the citizenry. World War II revisionism has yet to achieve this. It is still a mainly scholarly enterprise, confined for over a generation to a small number of specialists and their modest followings, and any effect it may have had on the general public is imperceptible. World War I revisionism had its moments of influence, also, on public policy in the interwar decades; that of World War II is, if anything, a negative and largely psychic quantity, gradually entering consciousness in the most subtle and sophisticated ways. Its preservation, therefore, as a literary tradition is still of primary concern, and the reedition of its best and most telling work serves this noble purpose well.

James J. Martin
January 1980   Colorado Springs

Revisionism:
A Key to Peace

Revisionism in Historical Writing

During the last forty years, revisionism has become a controversial term. To so-called revisionists, it implies an honest search for historical truth and the discrediting of misleading myths that may be a barrier to peace and goodwill among nations. In the minds of antirevisionists, the term often savors of mendacity, deviousness, malice, vindictiveness, and an unholy desire to smear the saviors of mankind. Actually, revisionism means nothing more or less than the effort to revise the historical record in the light of a more complete collection of historical facts, a more calm political atmosphere, and a more objective attitude.

In its origins, revisionism dates from the beginnings of historical writing in ancient oriental times in the historical books of the Bible. These were written and repeatedly revised over many centuries and it required about a century of study by expert biblical scholars in modern times to separate, however imperfectly, the original text from subsequent revisions. In the European tradition, historical writing starts with the Greeks, and the first true historian here was Hecataeus of Miletus (b. 500 B.C.), who is known chiefly as a revisionist of traditional Greek tales about Hellenic origins. As he put it: "What I write here is the account which I considered to be true: for the stories of the Greeks are numerous, and in my opinion ridiculous." The greatest scholar among Greek historians, Polybius, in his searching revisionist criticism of the use of sources by the Greek antiquarian Timaeus, was the first to lay down the fundamental principles of critical historical research and scholarship.

In the period of the Renaissance and humanism, Lorenzo Valla (1407–57) exposed the forged "Donation of Constantine," which was a cornerstone of the papal claim to secular power, and he later called attention to the unreliable methods of Livy in dealing with early Roman history. Much of the historical writing during the Reformation and Counter-Reformation was revisionist in nature, although often more heated than scholarly. In the cooperative work known as the *Magdeburg Centuries*, the Protestant historians attacked the accepted historical documents and dogmas of the Catholic church, and this was answered with equal revisionist vigor by Cardinal Baronius in his *Ecclesiastical Annals*. Revisionism has played a prominent role in historical writing from this time to the latest discussions of the causes of the Second World War.

Revisionism has been most frequently and effectively applied to correcting the historical record relative to wars because truth is always the first war casualty, the emotional disturbances and distortions in historical writing are greatest in wartime, and both the need and the material for correcting historical myths are most evident and profuse in connection with wars.

Revisionism was applied to the American Revolution many years ago. Beginning with the writings of men like George Louis Beer, and completed by the monumental work of Lawrence H. Gipson, it was shown that the British commercial policy toward the colonies was not as harsh and lawless as it had been portrayed by George Bancroft and others among the early ultrapatriotic historians. Others demonstrated that the British measures imposed on the colonies after the close of the French and Indian War were in general accord with the British constitutional system. Finally, Clarence W. Alvord made it clear that Britain was more concerned with the destiny of the area west of the Alleghenies than it was with such eastern coastwise disturbances as those connected with the Stamp Act, the Boston Massacre, and the Boston Tea Party.

The War of 1812 was similarly subjected to revisionist correction. Henry Adams revealed that Timothy Pickering and the extreme antiwar Federalists played a decisive role by indirectly encouraging the British to continue their oppressive commercial policies and their seizure of sailors on American ships that aided the American "warhawks" in leading this country into war. They misrepresented Jefferson's commercial and naval policies to an almost treasonable extent. More recently Irving Brant, in his notable biography of Madison, has argued that Madison was not actually pushed into war against his personal convictions by Clay,

Calhoun, and the "warhawks" but made the decision for war on the basis of his own beliefs.

The Mexican War has been effectively treated by revisionists. For a long time, historians who sought to correct the wartime passions of 1846 criticized Polk and the war group as rather conscienceless warmongers, impelled by political ambition, who pounced without justification upon a helpless little country. Then, in 1919, along came Justin H. Smith, who, in his *War With Mexico*, showed that there had been plenty of arrogance, defiance, and provocation on the part of Santa Ana and the Mexicans.

While the term revisionism has been little used in connection with the writings on this period, the causes of the Civil War (War between the States) have produced even more extensive revisionist research and restatement than the causes of either world war. This was made clear in the remarkable summary of revisionist interpretations of the coming of the Civil War by Professor Howard K. Beale in 1946, set forth in chapter iii of the monograph edited by Merle E. Curti, *Theory and Practice in Historical Study*. The outcome of these scholarly efforts demonstrated that the Civil War, like General Bradley's description of the Korean War, was "the wrong war, in the wrong place, at the wrong time." Hotheads on both sides brought on the war, while judicious restraint might easily have averted the catastrophe. Charles W. Ramsdell has suggested the interesting view that Lincoln actually executed a "Pearl Harbor" by inciting the South to strike the first blow through his reinforcement of Fort Sumter, thus anticipating Roosevelt's activities in all but forcing the Japanese to launch the Pacific war on December 7, 1941.

Professor William A. Dunning and his seminar students at Columbia University rigorously applied revisionism to the aftermath of the Civil War and the vindictive reconstruction measures piloted through Congress by Charles Sumner and Thaddeus Stevens. Their verdict was approved and popularized in Claude Bowers's book on *The Tragic Era*. Beginning in the 1930s a reaction set in against the revisionism by Dunning and his students. Today, under the leadership of historians such as Kenneth M. Stampp and T. Harry Williams, this reaction brands the interpretation of reconstruction by the Dunning school as a "myth." According to this revision of Dunning's revisionism, the northern radical Republicans, led by Stevens and Sumner, and the Negro leaders in the South were patriotic defenders of democracy and racial justice.

Revisionist historians soon tackled the propaganda concerning the Spanish-American War which had been fomented by Hearst and Pulitzer and showed how McKinley, with the Spanish concessions to his demands in his pocket, concealed the Spanish capitulation from Congress and demanded war. Further research has revealed that there is no conclusive evidence whatever that the Spanish sank the battleship *Maine*, and has shown that Theodore Roosevelt quite illegally started the war by an unauthorized order to Admiral Dewey to attack the Spanish fleet at Manila while Secretary Long was out of his office. The best revisionist presentation of the Spanish-American War was provided by Walter Millis in his *Martial Spirit* (1931). Julius H. Pratt and others have exposed the irresponsible warmongering of the "warhawks" of 1898, such as Theodore Roosevelt, Henry Cabot Lodge, and Albert J. Beveridge, and indicated the primary responsibility of Admiral Mahan for the expansionist philosophy upon which this rise of American imperialism was based.

Hence, long before the Austrian archduke was assassinated by Serbian plotters on June 28, 1914, revisionism had an impressive history and had been brought to bear on all the important wars in which the United States had been engaged. Applied abroad to the Franco-Prussian War, it clearly proved that the initiative lay with France rather than Bismarck and the Prussians. But it was the First World War which brought the term revisionism into general use.

Revisionism and the First World War

It is usually held that revisionism in connection with the First World War began a few years after the armistice of November 1918, but Harry Paxton Howard has done well to point out that it started *during* the war: "Actually, in the literal sense of the word, the biggest job of *revising* history was done during the First World War when our 'histories' were completely revised to show that Germany had always been our enemy, that Germany had started the war in 1914, that Germany had even started the Franco-Prussian War in 1870, and that in the Revolutionary War we had not really been fighting the British but the Hessians—not to mention such things as the Germans cutting the hands off Belgian babies, instead of the Belgians cutting off the hands of Congolese. This was a real revision of our histories which has distorted the American mind for over fifty years.''

By 1914 the new methods of communication, mass journalism, and greater mastery of propaganda techniques enabled the combatants to whip up popular opinion and mass hatred as never before in the history of warfare. Jonathan French Scott's *Five Weeks* revealed how the European press stirred up violent hatreds in July 1914. The intensity of feeling in the United States has been recalled in an impressive manner in H. C. Peterson's *Opponents of War, 1917-1918*. As C. Hartley Grattan, the present writer, and others have pointed out, the historians scrambled on the propaganda bandwagon with great alacrity and vehemence after April 1917. It was almost universally believed that Germany was entirely responsible not only for the outbreak of war in 1914 but also for American entry in April 1917. Anyone who publicly doubted this popular dogma was in danger of the tar bucket or worse. Eugene Debs was imprisoned by Wilson, who had proclaimed the war to be one to make the world safe for democracy. Debs's crime was a statement that the war had a primarily economic basis, precisely what Wilson himself declared in a speech on September 5, 1919.

There is no space here to go into the scope and nature of revisionist studies on the causes of the First World War. We can only illustrate the situation by citing a few of the outstanding myths and indicating the manner in which they were disposed of by revisionists.

The most damaging allegation brought against Germany was the charge that the kaiser called together a crown council of the leading German government officials, ambassadors, and financiers on July 5, 1914, revealed to them that he was about to throw Europe into war, and told them to get ready for the conflict. The financiers demanded two weeks' delay so as to be able to call in loans and sell securities. The kaiser acceded to this demand, and left the next day on a well-publicized vacation cruise. This was designed to lull England, France, and Russia into a false sense of security while Germany and Austria-Hungary secretly got ready to leap upon an unprepared and unsuspecting Europe. The first complete statement of these apparently damaging assertions appeared in *Ambassador Morgenthau's Story*, which was ghostwritten by a leading American journalist, Burton J. Hendrick.

Professor Sidney B. Fay, the leading American revisionist dealing with the outbreak of war in 1914, proved from the available documents in 1920 that this crown council legend was a complete myth. Some of the persons alleged to have been at the council meeting were not in Berlin at the time. The kaiser's actual attitude on July 5 was completely at variance with that portrayed in the legend, and there was no such financial action as was implied. But it was a long time before it was revealed how Mr. Morgenthau got this story. It was known that he was an honorable man, and not even the most severe critics of the myth charged that he had deliberately concocted and disseminated a lie of such proportions and profound implications.

Many years later, Paul Schwarz, who was the personal secretary to the German ambassador in Constantinople, Baron Hans von Wangenheim, revealed the facts. Von Wangenheim had a mistress in Berlin and, in the early days of the crisis of 1914, she demanded that he return at once to Berlin to settle some critical matters with her. He complied and, to conceal from his wife the real reason for his making the trip, he told her that the kaiser had suddenly summoned him to Berlin. On his return, he told his wife about the fanciful crown council that he had dreamed up. Shortly after this, with his wife by his side, von Wangenheim met Morgenthau, then the American ambassador at Constantinople, at a diplomatic reception. Morgenthau had heard about von Wangenheim's trip to Berlin and inquired of him as to what had happened. Under the circumstances, von Wangenheim was under pressure to repeat the myth he had told his wife. To what extent liquor may have stimulated his imagination or lessened his restraint, and how much Morgenthau and Hendrick elaborated on what von Wangenheim actually told Morgenthau, are not known and probably never will be.

This fantastic tale, created out of whole cloth, both indicates the need for revisionism and demonstrates how momentous and tragic events may hang on the most palpable fabrications. Since Morgenthau's book did not appear until 1918, the recency and sensational nature of his tale about the fictitious crown council had a great influence upon Allied propaganda against Germany at the end of the war. It was used in Lloyd George's campaign of

1918 advocating the hanging of the kaiser and exploited by the more vindictive makers of the Treaty of Versailles. It is quite possible that, otherwise, the latter would never have been able to write the fateful war-guilt clause into the treaty. Since historians are agreed that it was the Treaty of Versailles which prepared the way for the Second World War, the harebrained von Wangenheim alibi of July 1914, may have had some direct relation to the sacrifice of millions of lives and astronomical expenditures of money in the wars since 1939, with the possibility that the ultimate consequences may be the extermination of much of the human race through nuclear warfare.

Another item which was used to inflame opinion against the Germans was their invasion of Belgium. The Allied propaganda presented this as the main reason for the entry of England into the war and the final proof of the charge that the Germans had no regard for international law or the rights of small nations. Revisionist scholars proved that the British and French had for some time been considering the invasion of Belgium in the event of a European war, and that English officers had traveled over Belgium carefully surveying the terrain against this contingency. Further, the Germans offered to respect the neutrality of Belgium in return for British neutrality in the war. Finally, John Burns, one of the two members of the British cabinet who resigned when Britain made the decision for war in 1914, told me personally in the summer of 1927 that the cabinet decision for war had definitely been made before a word had been said about the Belgian issue. The following year, the *Memorandum on Resignation* of the famed John Morley, the other cabinet member who resigned in 1914 as a protest against the war policy, fully confirmed Burns's account of the matter. The facts brought forth by Burns, Morley, and others as to the myth that England decided to go to war because of the German invasion of Belgium are confirmed by the latest British book on 1914, George M. Thomson's *Twelve Days* (1964), written to commemorate the fiftieth anniversary of the outbreak of the First World War. Thomson makes it clear that the most ardent, determined, and ubiquitous British warmonger in 1914 was Winston Churchill, then first lord of the admiralty.

A third leading allegation which produced violent feelings against the Germans in the First World War was the charge that they had committed unique and brutal atrocities against civilians, especially in Belgium—mutilating children, women, and the helpless, generally. They were said to have utilized the bodies of dead German and Allied soldiers to make fertilizers and soap, and otherwise to have behaved like degraded beasts. The distinguished British publicist Lord James Bryce was induced to lend his name to the authentication of these atrocity reports. After the war, a large number of books riddled these atrocity tales, notably Sir Arthur Ponsonby's *Falsehood in Wartime,* and J. M. Read's *Atrocity Propaganda.* When Bryce was queried on this matter by the brilliant English lawyer and publicist Irene Cooper Willis, he only shrugged his shoulders and said: "You know how things go in wartime!" The First World War was no picnic but no honest and informed scholar today believes that any considerable part of the alleged atrocities actually took place or that the Germans were any more guilty of atrocious conduct than other participants in the war.

Scholars and publicists who had been condemned to silence during the war soon sought to clear their consciences and set the record straight after the close of hostilities. Indeed, Francis Neilson anticipated many basic revisionist conclusions in his *How Diplomats Make War,* which was published in 1915 and may be regarded as the first important revisionist book on the causes of the First World War. Lord Loreburn's *How the War Came,* a scathing indictment of the English diplomats of 1914, came out at the same time that the Treaty of Versailles was drafted.

Only the briefest summary can be given here of the revisionist conclusions relative to the entry of the United States into the First World War. There had been a notable shift in the American attitude toward Germany between 1870 and 1915. At the former date, we were more friendly toward Germany than toward any other European state, but even before war broke out in 1914 we were more hostile in our attitude toward Germany than toward any other main European country. This transformation was due in part to trade rivalries and clashes in imperialistic ventures, but even more to the fact that American news and comments concerning Germany in the decade before 1914 came primarily through the notoriously anti-German Harmsworth (Northcliffe) papers.

Woodrow Wilson, unlike Franklin D. Roosevelt, was a man who preferred peace to war. Even though Wilson's cultural sympathies with respect to foreign countries were overwhelmingly pro-British, he quite sincerely called for a neutral attitude on the part of this country and did maintain neutrality for some time after the outbreak of war. There is no doubt, in the light of the latest evidence, that he wished to mediate between the warring powers and bring the bloody conflict to an end. A conversation he had with a famous American editor, Frank I. Cobb of the New York *World,* the night before he delivered his war message on April 7, 1917, shows that even then he had much hesitation about bringing the country into war. But there were just too many persons, forces, and factors favorable to war for him to control.

Colonel House, Secretary Lansing, and Ambassador Page in London, undermined Wilson's peace efforts even to the point of sheer betrayal and insubordination. Grotesque exaggerations of alleged German atrocities in the Bryce report and elsewhere made most Americans believe that the Germans were a brutal and ruthless people. This propaganda was extended to the religious realm in the bellicose sermons of Newell Dwight Hillis and others who proclaimed the conflict to be a "holy war." Bankers who had made large loans to Britain and France encouraged American entry, as did businessmen who envisaged the large profits in producing war materiel. The sinking of the *Lusitania,* which now appears to have been accomplished with the connivance of Churchill and the British authorities, helped to spur American indignation over alleged German ruthlessness. Lansing and Page made it all but impossible to keep England restrained to the international law of war, while it was insisted that Germany be held to "strict accountability." When Wilson, as Professor Link has recently revealed, made a sincere effort to mediate in Europe and bring peace right after his reelection in 1916, Lansing treacherously betrayed him by urging the Allies to insist on terms that the Germans could not accept unless they were willing to admit defeat. The Germans were left with no alternative except unrestricted submarine warfare, which became the final rationalized justification for the decision to put the United States into the war. When the inevitable results of this policy eventuated in the Treaty of Versailles, Lansing became one of the chief critics of the situation which he had probably done more than any other American to bring about. To a very considerable extent, the war was Lansing's war rather than Wilson's.

The first American scholar thoroughly to challenge the wartime propaganda was Professor Sidney B. Fay of Smith College, who brought out a series of three striking articles in the *American Historical Review,* beginning in July 1920. These first aroused my interest in the facts. During the war, I had accepted the anti-German propaganda; indeed, had unwittingly written some of it. While I wrote some reviews and short articles dealing with the actual causes of the First World War between 1921 and 1924, I first got thoroughly involved in the revisionist struggle when Herbert Croly of the *New Republic* induced me in March 1924 to review at length the book of Professor Charles Downer Hazen, *Europe Since 1815.* This aroused so much controversy that George W. Ochs-Oakes, editor of the *New York Times Current History Magazine,* urged me to set forth a summary of revisionist conclusions at the time in the issue of May 1924. This really launched the revisionist battle on the public level in the United States.

Very soon even the largest publishing houses and the best periodicals eagerly sought revisionist material for publication. Professor Fay's *Origins of the World War,* J. S. Ewart's *Roots and Causes of the Wars,* my *Genesis of the World War,* and Frederick Bausman's *Let France Explain* were the leading revisionist books on 1914 by American authors published in the United States. American revisionists found allies in Europe: Georges Demartial, Alfred Fabre-Luce, and others, in France; Friedrich Stieve, Max Montgelas, Alfred von Wegerer, Hermann Lutz, and others, in Germany; and G. P. Gooch, Raymond Beazley, and G. Lowes Dickinson, in England. Turning from the causes of war in Europe in 1914, other scholars, notably Charles C. Tansill, Walter Millis, C. Hartley Grattan, and John K. Turner told the truth about the entry of the United States into the war. Mauritz Hallgren produced the definitive indictment of American interventionist diplomacy from Wilson to Roosevelt in his *Tragic Fallacy.*

At the outset, American revisionist writing was somewhat precarious. Professor Fay was not in peril, personally, for he wrote in a scholarly journal which the public missed or ignored. But when I began to deal with the subject in media read by at least the upper intellectual level of the "men on the street," it was a different matter. I recall giving a lecture in Trenton, New Jersey, in the early days of revisionism and being threatened bodily by fanatics who were present. They were cowed and discouraged by the chairman of the evening, who happened to be a much respected former governor of New Jersey. Even in the autumn of 1924, a rather scholarly audience in Amherst, Massachusetts, became somewhat agitated and was only calmed down when Ray Stannard Baker expressed general agreement with my remarks.

Gradually, the temper of the country changed, but at first it was caused more by resentment against our former allies than by the impact of revisionist writings. It was the "Uncle Shylock" talk of 1924–27 which turned the trick. This indication of implied Allied ingratitude for American aid in the war made the public willing to read and accept the truth relative to the causes, conduct, merits, and results of the First World War. Moreover, with the passage of time, the intense emotions of wartime had an opportunity to cool off. By the mid-1930s, when Walter Millis's *Road to War* appeared, it was welcomed by a great mass of American readers and was one of the most successful books of the decade. Revisionism had finally won out.

Interestingly enough, as a phase of the violent antirevisionism after 1945, there has set in a determined effort on the part of some historians and journalists to discredit the revisionist scholarship of 1920–39 and return to the myths of 1914–20. This has even taken place in West Germany in such examples as the fantastic writings of Fritz Fischer of Hamburg, who claims to have found evidence that the German leaders in 1914 had dreams of gains and annexations in the event of a German victory. This may well be true, but it was also the case with the leaders on both sides. Fischer writes as though he had never heard of the secret treaties of the Allies. This trend to bypass World War I revisionism is devastatingly challenged and refuted by the eminent expert on World War I revisionism Hermann Lutz, in his book on *German-French Unity* (1957), which takes account of recent materials in the field.

As we have already explained briefly, the historical scholarship that sought to produce the truth relative to the causes of the First World War came to be known as revisionism. The Treaty of Versailles had been directly based on the thesis of the unique and sole German-Austrian responsibility for the coming of the war in 1914. By the mid-1920s, scholars had established the fact that Russia, France, and Serbia were more responsible than Germany and Austria. Hence, from the standpoint of both political logic and factual material, the treaty should have been revised in accordance with the newly revealed truth. Nothing of the sort took place, and in 1933 Hitler appeared on the scene to carry out the revision of Versailles on a unilateral basis, with the result that another and more devastating world war broke out in 1939.

Since revisionism, whatever its services to the cause of historical truth, failed to avert the Second World War, many have regarded the effort to seek the truth about the responsibility for war as futile in any practical sense. But any such conclusion is not convincing. Had not the general political and economic situation in Europe, from 1920 onward, been such as overwhelmingly to encourage emotions and restrain reason, there is every probability that the revisionist verdict on 1914 would have led to changes in the Versailles *diktat* that might have preserved peace. In the United States, less disturbed by emotional crosscurrents, revisionism exerted an impressive influence which worked for peace. It was partly responsible for increasing the restraint imposed on France at the time of the Ruhr invasion, for the mitigation of the harsh reparations program, for the Nye investigation of the armament industry and its nefarious ramifications, and for our neutrality legislation.

The fact that, despite many months of the most vigorous and irresponsible propaganda for our intervention in the Second World War, over 80 percent of the American people were in favor of refraining from intervention on the very eve of Pearl Harbor proves that the impact of revisionism on the American public mind had been deep, abiding, and salutary. If President Roosevelt had not been able to incite the Japanese to attack Pearl Harbor, the revisionist campaign of the late 1920s might have saved the United States from the tragedies of 1941–45 and the calamities which have already grown out of our intervention in the Second World War, to say nothing of the more appalling disasters that may still lie ahead of us.

Revisionism and the Second World War

Greater hatreds and more ruthless propaganda

Long before the Second World War broke out at the beginning of September 1939, it was evident that, when it came, it would present an even more dramatic and formidable revisionist problem at its close than did the First World War. The stage was all set for a much greater volume and variety of distorting hatreds than in the years before 1914, and the capacity to whip up passion and disseminate myths had notably increased in the interval. Many technical advances in journalism, larger newspaper staffs, especially of foreign "experts," and greater emphasis on foreign affairs, all made it certain that the press would play a far more effective role in swaying the masses than in 1914–19. Indeed, even in 1914, as Jonathan F. Scott and Oron J. Hale have made clear, the press was perhaps as potent a cause of the war as the folly of the heads of states and their diplomats. It was bound to exert an even more powerful and malevolent influence in 1939 and thereafter.

The techniques of propaganda had been enormously improved and were well-nigh completely removed from any moral restraint. The propagandists in 1939 and thereafter had at their disposal not only what had been learned relative to lying to the public during the First World War but also the impressive advances made in the techniques of public deceit for both civilian and military purposes after 1918. A leading English intelligence officer, Sidney Rogerson, even wrote a book, published in 1938, *Propaganda in the Next War,* in which he told his fellow Englishmen how to handle Americans in the case of a Second World War, warning them that they could not just use over again the methods which Sir Gilbert Parker and others had so successfully employed from 1914 to 1918 to beguile the American public. He suggested new myths and strategy which would be needed.

These new methods were worked out and applied after war broke out in 1939. They were not of the genteel and persuasive type followed by Sir Gilbert Parker but were of a ruthless and irresponsible nature which should have made Rogerson gasp with astonishment, and were carried on not only with the connivance but the active assistance of prominent American officials such as J. Edgar Hoover and Colonel "Wild Bill" Donovan. They were directed by Sir William Stephenson, "the quiet Canadian," and are described in a book under this title by H. Montgomery Hyde. It was literally an invasion of the United States by a British fifth column. Had Stephenson and his associates been Germans, they would have been summarily seized and presumably imprisoned if not shot. When some American citizens showed rather extreme zeal in opposing American entry into the war, they were arrested and subjected to a sedition trial which was probably the most serious challenge to liberty since the alien and sedition laws at the end of the eighteenth century. The Orwellian nature of the postwar situation was underlined by the fact that the man who was formally responsible for the trial was later made the national president of the American Civil Liberties Committee. When Parker's methods of 1914–18 were revealed, they produced a considerable wave of criticism, even revulsion, in many American circles. But when Hyde's book was published in England and soon issued in an American edition as *Room 3603,* there was not even a ripple of criticism. It passed virtually unnoticed save for occasional commendation.

There was a far greater backlog of bitter hatreds for the propagandists to play upon by 1939. However much the kaiser was lampooned and reviled during the war, he had been rather highly regarded before July 1914. In 1913, at the time of the twenty-fifth anniversary of his accession to the throne, such leading Americans as Theodore Roosevelt, Nicholas Murray Butler, and former President Taft praised the kaiser lavishly. Butler contended that if he had been born in the United States he would have been put in the White House without the formality of an election, and Taft stated that the kaiser had been the greatest single force for peace in the whole world during his entire reign.

There were no such sentiments of affection and admiration held in reserve for Hitler and Mussolini in 1939. Butler had, indeed, called Mussolini the greatest statesman of the twentieth century. Churchill had declared that if he had been an Italian he would have been "wholeheartedly with Mussolini from start to finish." While these statements by Butler and Churchill were made in the late 1920s, Churchill referred to Mussolini in 1935 as "so great a man and so wise a leader." About the same time, he was paying comparable compliments to Hitler, but he promptly forgot about these tributes when war broke out in 1939. British propaganda against Il Duce during the Ethiopian foray had put an end to most American admiration of him. The hatred built up against Hitler in the democracies by 1939 already exceeded that massed against any other public figure in modern history. American and British conservatives hated Stalin and the Communists, and they were later linked with Germany and Hitler after the Russo-German pact of August 1939. This hatred of the Russians was fanned to a whiter flame when they invaded eastern Poland in the autumn of 1939 and Finland during the following winter. Racial differences and the color bogey made it easy to hate the Japanese and, after the attack on Pearl Harbor, the real facts about which were not to be known until after the war, the hatred of the Japanese went so far that even leading American naval officers like Admiral William F. Halsey could refer to the Japanese as literally subhuman anthropoids.

Against this background it was obvious that hatreds could thrive "without stint or limit," to use Mr. Wilson's phrase, and that lies could arise and luxuriate with abandon and without any effort to check on the facts, if there were any. Every leading country set up its official agency to carry on public deception for the duration and supported it lavishly with almost unlimited funds. It was more than evident that it would be a formidable task for revisionism to wrestle with the war propaganda once hostilities had ended.

Historical writing on the Second World War

After the First World War, the Russians took the first important steps in launching revisionism. The Communists wished to discredit the czarist regime and saddle it with responsibility for the First World War, so they published the voluminous documents containing the secret Franco-Russian agreements from 1892 to 1914. These, together with supplementary French materials, did prove that France, Russia, and Serbia were mainly responsible for the outbreak of war in 1914. The publication of the Russian documents was soon followed by the appearance of those of Germany and Austria, and in due time the British, French, and Italians offered considerable access to their archives. I have already indicated that many important revisionist books appeared in European countries.

Following the Second World War, the overwhelming majority of revisionist writings have been produced in the United States. There was no czar for the Russians to blame in 1945. Stalin desired to preserve intact the legend that his "collective security" formula, which Litvinov sold to the popular front nations and to liberals generally, proved his desire for peace and that he had been surprised and betrayed by the German attack on June 22, 1941. England was watching her empire disintegrate, and the British leaders were aware of the primary responsibility of Britain for the outbreak of war in 1939; hence, every effort was made to discourage revisionist writing in England. Chamberlain and Halifax were presented as being determined appeasers to the bitter end in early September 1939. Only A. J. P. Taylor produced a forthright book on the causes of the Second World War. France was torn with hatreds even worse than those of the French Revolution, and about one hundred thousand Frenchmen were butchered either directly or quasi-legally during the "liberation." Only the famous journalist Sisley Huddleston, an expatriate Englishman resident in France, the distinguished publicist Alfred Fabre-Luce, the able journalist Maurice Bardèche, the implacable Jacques Benoist-Mechin, and the courageous French historian and geographer Paul Rassinier produced anything that savored of revisionism in France.

Germany and Italy, under the heels of conquerors for years, were in no position to launch revisionist studies. Even when Germany was freed, the hatred of Hitler which had survived the war and political pressure, especially from the United States and Israel, discouraged revisionist work. For some years, only Hans Grimm and Ernst von Salomon produced anything resembling revisionism in Germany, and their works were not devoted primarily to diplomatic history. During the 1950s, however, West German publicists and historians gained some new courage and determination, in part due to encouragement from the revisionist books by non-Germans, mainly Americans, which were translated and published in Germany. In the late 1950s and in the early 1960s a number of worthy German revisionist books made their appearance.

The more important German revisionist works are the interpretation of political leadership in the Western world between the two world wars by Edmund Marhefka, a delegate to the Versailles conference and one of the first to repudiate sole German responsibility for the Second World War; Udo Walendy's able statement concerning the need for a truthful account of recent world history and responsibility for the Second World War; Willi Glasebock's extended and well-documented attack upon the thesis of the Allies and the Bonn government that Germany was solely responsible for the Second World War; the comprehensive two-volume work of Friedrich Lenz, *Never Again Munich,* which is far the best contribution of a Germanic writer to the revisionist study of the causes of the Second World War, and is worthy to rank with the books of Stieve, Montgelas, Von Wegerer, and Lutz in the revisionist literature on the First World War; Erich Kern's account of how the Versailles Treaty and European diplomacy after 1920 led to the rise of Hitler and national socialism; Helmut Sundermann's works on the Anglo-American encouragement of the Second World War, the nature of the Third Reich, and the background and results of the Potsdam conference; C. J. Burckhardt's presentation of the Danzig question as preliminary to the outbreak of war in 1939; Philipp Fabry's analysis of the Stalin-Hitler Pact of August 1939, and Heinrich Hartle's extended study of German and Allied responsibility for the Second World War, including a searching analysis of the Nuremberg trials. A good summary of German revisionist writing on the Second World War has been provided by Walther Reitenhart. Two substantial German journals publishing revisionist materials have been firmly launched: *Nation Europa,* edited by Arthur Ehrhardt, and *Deutschen Hochschullehrer-Zeitung,* edited by Herbert Grabert.

In Italy, the eminent scholar and diplomatic historian Luigi Villari wrote an able book on the foreign policy of Mussolini which is one of the substantial products of revisionism on the Second World War, but he had to get his book published in the United States. The same was true of his book on the "liberation" of Italy after 1943.

In the United States, revisionism got off to an early start and flourished relatively, so far as the production of substantial books was concerned, despite the fact that not one large commercial publisher in the United States has published an important revisionist book since Pearl Harbor, and revisionist literature has been made available mainly by some two small courageous publishers. This relative profusion of revisionist volumes was, however, far surpassed by the almost insuperable obstacles that were met in trying to make such literature known to the public and read by it. In other words, an unprecedented volume of revisionist books was accompanied by an even more formidable "historical blackout" that has thus far been able to conceal most of the revisionist material from the reading public.

The reasons for the relatively greater productivity of revisionism in the United States for a decade after 1945 are not difficult to discover. There had been over four years of debate about the European and world situation between President Roosevelt's Chicago bridge speech in October 1937 and the Japanese attack on Pearl Harbor on December 7, 1941. Most of the men who produced revisionist books after 1945 had taken part in this great debate, had gathered materials on the issues, and were well aware of the realities and of the misinformation spread by the interventionists. They were eager to come forth with books to sustain their position as soon as the end of hostilities made this possible. Pearl Harbor had silenced them only for the duration. Further, the United States had been untouched by the ravages of war, it was in good economic condition at V-J Day, and it had not lost any colonial possessions. Four years of vigorous debate before Pearl Harbor and nearly four years of passionate lying and hating after that date had at least slightly restrained the American capacity for hatred for the time being, as compared with the existing situation in Europe and Asia. While not at all comparable to the situation after 1918, there was at least a slight and brief breathing spell until hatreds were revived when Truman launched the cold war in March 1947.

We have space to mention only some outstanding revisionist products in the United States dealing with the Second World War. John T. Flynn's *As We Go Marching* was published in 1944, his pioneer brochures on Pearl Harbor in 1944 and 1945, and his *Roosevelt Myth* in 1948. George Morgenstern's *Pearl Harbor* appeared in 1947; Charles Austin Beard's two volumes on Roosevelt's foreign policy were brought out in 1946 and 1948; and Helen Mears's *Mirror for Americans: Japan* came out in 1948. William Henry Chamberlin's *America's Second Crusade* was published in 1950; Frederic R. Sanborn's *Design for War* came off the presses in 1951; Charles C. Tansill's *Back Door to War* made its appearance in 1952; the symposium *Perpetual War for Perpetual Peace,* which I edited and which presents the best anthology of revisionist conclusions on the Second World War, came out in the summer of 1953; and Richard N. Current's *Secretary Stimson* was published in 1954. Admiral R. A. Theobald's *Final Secret of Pearl Harbor* also appeared in 1954; René A. Wormser's *Myth of the Good and Bad Nations* and Francis Neilson's *Churchill Legend* came out in this same year; Admiral H. E. Kimmel's *Admiral Kimmel's Story* was published in 1955; Bryton Barron's *Inside the State Department* was brought out in 1956; George N. Crocker's

Roosevelt's Road to Russia was issued in 1959; Anne Armstrong's *Unconditional Surrender* appeared in 1961; William L. Neumann's *America Encounters Japan* was published in 1963; and James J. Martin's massive two-volume work, *American Liberalism and World Politics, 1931–1941,* appeared in 1965.

In addition to these books by American revisionists, there was an impressive list of volumes by Europeans who sought to escape the even more stringent historical blackout at home and secure respectable publication and publicity in the United States. Such were: Hermann Lutz's *Franco-German Unity;* Sisley Huddleston's books on *Popular Diplomacy and War* and *France: the Tragic Years;* the trenchant criticisms of the war-crimes trials by Lord Hankey and Montgomery Belgion; the remarkable book of F. J. P. Veale, *Advance to Barbarism,* which criticized both the barbarous saturation bombing of civilians and the war-crimes trials; Russell Grenfell's devastating exposure of Germanophobia in his *Unconditional Hatred;* Emrys Hughes's brilliant biographical study of Winston Churchill; Charles Bewley's substantial and authoritative biography of Hermann Goering; and Dr. Villari's volumes on Mussolini's foreign policy and the Allied liberation of Italy.

There were a number of other American books on the periphery of literal revisionism, of which Freda Utley's *High Cost of Vengeance,* dealing with the Allied folly and barbarism in Germany after V-E Day, and Nicholas Balabkins's *Germany Under Direct Controls,* treating the application of the revised Morgenthau Plan to postwar Germany, are representative and among the more notable. Along with them might be mentioned such books as Andy Rooney and Bud Hutton's *Conqueror's Peace;* Marshall Knappen's *And Call It Peace;* Milton Mayer's *They Thought They Were Free;* Harold Zink's *American Military Government in Germany;* and John T. Snell's *Wartime Origins of the East-West Dilemna Over Germany.*

It has been maintained by some commentators friendly with revisionism that what is really needed today are more and better revisionist books. But the preceding information makes it clear that there has been no dearth of good books presenting the revisionist case relative to the Second World War, except for the responsibility for the outbreak of war in 1939. But this gap was filled by A. J. P. Taylor's *Origins of the Second World War,* which appeared in 1961. As will be made clear later on, the problem has not been one of a lack of adequate and reliable books but the almost insuperable difficulties in getting these books presented effectively to the scholarly and intelligent general public.

Some leading revelations of revisionism bearing on the
Second World War

Not only have there been many more formidable revisionist volumes published in the United States since 1945 than in the comparable period after 1918, but the facts revealed by this recent revisionist research have been far more sensational than those produced by revisionist scholars after the First World War.

From 1937 onward, Stalin had worked as hard for a war of attrition and mutual destruction between the capitalistic Nazi, fascist, and democratic countries as Sazonov and Izvolski did in 1914 to start a Franco-Russian-English war against Germany and Austria.

Hitler, far from precipitately launching an aggressive war against Poland on the heels of brutal and unreasonable demands, made a greater effort to avert war during the August 1939 crisis than the kaiser did during the crisis of July 1914. And Hitler's demands on Poland were the most reasonable ones he made on any foreign country during his whole regime. They were far more conciliatory than Stresemann and the Weimar republic would even consider. Poland was far more unreasonable and intransigent in 1938–39 than Serbia had been in 1914. Hitler became involved in war more because of inability to cope with the devious diplomacy of Halifax than because of bellicose intent. He allowed himself to be trapped into occupying Prague by the British indications that there would not be any serious objections to this move. Then the British sprang Halifax's trap by alleging that Hitler's occupation of Prague was a ruthless violation of his promises at Munich and an indication that he aimed at world conquest. This clever but devious move, combined with a false charge by Virgil Tilea, the Rumanian minister in London, that Germany had just sent an ultimatum to Rumania, was used to justify Chamberlain's hasty and precipitate guarantee to Poland at the end of March 1939, which Halifax and Chamberlain realized almost inevitably meant a new European war. Hitler failed to defeat this stratagem by sitting tight and consolidating his new position, resources, and strength. His proposals to Poland were just and moderate but it was not necessary to enter a second British trap by military action against Poland. Like Berchtold in 1914, Hitler failed to read the British mind in respect to foreign policy.

Mussolini sought to dissuade Hitler from going to war in 1939, and made repeated efforts to summon peace conferences after the war began. Far from wantonly sticking "a dagger in the back of France" in June 1940, he was virtually forced into the war by un-neutral acts of economic strangulation on the part of Britain. France was loath to go to war in 1939, and only extreme pressure by the British foreign office prodded Bonnet and Daladier into reluctantly acceding to the bellicose British policy on September 2–3, 1939.

Whereas, in 1914, British responsibility for the First World War was chiefly that of weakness and duplicity on the part of Sir Edward Grey—more a negative than a positive responsibility—the British were almost solely responsible in any direct sense for the outbreak of both the German-Polish and the European wars in early September 1939. Lord Halifax, the British foreign minister, who really directed British foreign policy from March to September, 1939, and Sir Howard Kennard, the British ambassador in Warsaw, were as responsible for the European war of 1939 as Sazonov, Izvolski, and Poincaré were for that of 1914. Chamberlain's speech before parliament on the night of September 2, 1939, was as mendacious a misrepresentation of the German position as had been Sir Edward Grey's address to parliament on August 3, 1914.

The plain fact is that Britain had decided upon war by March 1939 for the purpose of preserving the balance of power on the continent of Europe, which had been the fundamental item in British foreign policy since the days of Cardinal Wolsey in the sixteenth century. Hitler's unexpected success in revising the Treaty of Versailles and the equally sensational success of Goering in rebuilding the German economy had made Germany so strong that the British leaders believed that the balance of power was in mortal danger. Churchill put the matter in a nutshell when, only about a year after Churchill had paid Hitler what Francis Neilson described as the most glowing tribute ever given by a prominent

Englishman to the head of a foreign state, he told General Robert E. Wood in November 1936 that "Germany is getting too strong and we must smash her." Churchill's views were warmly seconded by his outstanding American friend and intimate, Bernard Baruch, who remarked to General George C. Marshall in 1938: "We are going to lick that fellow Hitler. He isn't going to get away with it." Even after his talk with General Wood, Churchill publicly stated that if England ever got into the same sorry situation as Germany had found itself in 1933 he hoped that England would find her Hitler to solve the problems England faced.

The antirevisionists have especially attacked the Munich conference and agreement as one of the most evil episodes in human history, notably in recent years when the facts might compel a more reasonable attitude toward Hitler's conduct a year later. The actual nature of this historic event is realistically described by A. J. P. Taylor, who has produced the only thorough and reliable treatment of the causes of the Second World War in the English language: "The settlement at Munich was a triumph for British policy, which had worked precisely to this end; not a triumph for Hitler, who had started with no such clear intention.... It was a triumph for all that was best and most enlightened in British life; a triumph for those who had preached equal justice among peoples; a triumph for those who had courageously denounced the harshness and shortsightedness of Versailles."

President Roosevelt had a major responsibility, both direct and indirect, for the outbreak of war in Europe. He began to exert pressure on France to stand up to Hitler as early as the German reoccupation of the Rhineland in March 1936, months before he was making his strongly isolationist speeches in the campaign of 1936. This pressure on France, and also England, continued right down to the coming of the war in September 1939. It gained volume and momentum after the quarantine speech of October 1937. As the crisis approached between Munich and the outbreak of war, Roosevelt pressed the Poles to stand firm against any demands by Germany, and urged the English and French to back up the Poles unflinchingly. From captured Polish and French archives, the Germans collected no less than five volumes of material consisting almost exclusively of Roosevelt's bellicose pressure on European countries, mainly France and Poland. The Allies later seized them. Only a small portion has ever been published, most notably some seized by the Germans in Poland in 1939 and published as the *German White Paper*. It is possible that the material covering Roosevelt's pressure on England might amount to more than five volumes. There is grave doubt that England would have gone to war in September 1939, had it not been for Roosevelt's encouragement and his assurances that, in the event of war, the United States would enter on the side of Britain just as soon as he could swing American public opinion around to support intervention. Yet, when the crisis became acute after August 23, 1939, Roosevelt sent several messages *for the record* urging that war be avoided through negotiations.

In regard to American entry into the European war, the case against President Roosevelt is far more serious than that against Woodrow Wilson with respect to the First World War. Wilson remained neutral for some time after 1914, and Professor Arthur S. Link has recently revealed that after his reelection in 1916 Wilson made a serious and honest effort to mediate between the contending European powers and suggest reasonable terms of peace. But these efforts were frustated by the treachery of Secretary of State Robert Lansing and came to naught. Roosevelt had abandoned all semblance of neutrality, even before the war broke out in 1939, and moved as speedily as was safe and feasible in the face of an anti-interventionist American public to involve this country in the European conflict.

The statement of Clare Booth Luce that Roosevelt lied the United States into war was one of the most restrained understatements of the wartime period. While he was publicly insisting that he favored peace and was assuring American fathers and mothers that their sons would not be sent into any foreign wars, he was actually engaged in secret intrigue with Winston Churchill planning how the United States might rapidly be brought into the war in behalf of Britain and France. Beginning even before war broke out in Europe, Roosevelt and Hull began an unbroken series of acts and policies hostile to Japan until they were finally able to provoke the Japanese to attack Pearl Harbor.

On July 26, 1939, Hull informed the Japanese that the American commercial treaty with Japan would be abrogated in six months, and in December 1939 a moral embargo was invoked against the shipment of vital raw materials to Japan. In 1940 Roosevelt put through the first peacetime draft in our history, arranged the "destroyer deal" which legally put the country at war, and appointed the two leading Republican interventionists, Henry L. Stimson and Frank Knox, as secretary of war and secretary of the navy, respectively. This was done to give an ostensible bipartisan cast to his drive for war. Stimson immediately began to work for a stiffer embargo policy against Japan. Early in 1940, at the suggestion of the British and against the advice of the chief of naval operations and the commander in chief of the Pacific fleet, the fleet was sent to Pearl Harbor, where the ships were bottled up like sitting ducks as a target in the event of a Japanese attack. Joint staff conferences with the British began in December 1940 and continued until April 1941, one outcome of which was Roosevelt's promise that the United States would make war on Japan if Japanese forces went beyond an arbitrary line in the South Pacific, even though the Japanese did not attack the American flag or forces. Admiral Stark then informed his commanders that it was only a question of time and place in regard to American entry into the war. This agreement with the English was a direct betrayal of Roosevelt's campaign promises and of the Democratic platform of 1940 which pledged no war unless attacked.

All during 1941, until the attack on Pearl Harbor on December 7, Roosevelt kept assuring the American public, which was still overwhelmingly against intervention, that all his actions were "short of war," but throughout this year he also performed one deed after another that made American entry into the war more certain and more imminent. In January 1941 he sent Harry Hopkins to London to assure Churchill that the United States was in the war with Britain to a victorious end. Beginning in May, stringent economic and financial pressure was launched against Japan which American civil and military leaders recognized would mean certain war since they involved the economic strangulation of Japan and offered her no alternative except war or collapse. Philippine exports to Japan were banned by executive order on May 29, 1941, and on July 26, 1941, all Japanese assets in the United States were frozen and all American trade with Japan brought to a summary end. The Lend-Lease Act was put through in March 1941 and was immediately followed by the convoying of ships taking supplies to Britain, hoping that the convoying vessels would be fired on by the Germans or Italians, thus giving Roosevelt his impatiently awaited opportunity to enter the conflict directly.

When these countries failed to rise to the bait and provide a *casus belli* in the Atlantic, Roosevelt met with Churchill in Newfoundland on August 9 and formulated a program to force Japan to attack the United States and thus enable the latter to enter the war through the Japanese "back door." Beginning as early as January 1941 Roosevelt rejected the repeated and substantial Japanese overtures for peaceful arrangements, although he was urged to give them careful consideration by Joseph C. Grew, the American ambassador in Tokyo. Against the advice of General Marshall and Admiral Stark, he brushed aside the proposal of a *modus vivendi* and approved Secretary Hull's sending an ultimatum to Japan on November 26 which Hull admitted meant the end of diplomacy and the coming of war in a matter of days.

The Japanese peace overtures were remarkable, almost urgent. Japan twice offered to get out of the Rome-Berlin-Tokyo Axis in return for peaceful arrangements with the United States. In January 1941 the Japanese suggested willingness to retire from their drive into China and southeast Asia as the price of peace with the United States. In March the Japanese ambassador in Washington began some forty fruitless conferences with Hull to secure a peaceful settlement with the United States. In August Prince Konoye, the Japanese prime minister, made the astonishing concession of agreeing to meet Roosevelt at any designated place to work out some method of preserving peace between the two countries. He agreed to accept in advance, as the basis for negotiations, the four fundamental principles laid down by Hull in April 1941 as an adequate basis for the settlement of Japanese-American relations. Even after this amazing proposal was curtly turned down, the Japanese made remarkable overtures for peace in November 1941 and sent Saburo Kurusu, well known as a friend of the United States and an expert on Japanese-American relations, to Washington to assist the Japanese ambassador in the negotiations. Even when the Japanese fleet started for Pearl Harbor it had orders to turn back if the United States indicated any evidence of willingness substantially to modify Hull's ultimatum. While Hull denounced the Japanese reply to his ultimatum on December 7 in very explosive and colorful language, it was actually a very moderate and reasonably accurate summary of Japanese-American relations, considering the source and the conditions of the moment.

It had been assumed in American naval strategy that, in the event of a Japanese attack on the United States, they would start out with a surprise attack on an American fleet if it were based in the Pacific. American naval maneuvers had shown that it would be feasible to make a surprise attack on Pearl Harbor launched as close as one hundred miles away. This was one reason why Admiral Richardson opposed bottling up the fleet at Pearl Harbor. In 1941 this danger would appear to have been largely overlooked. Not even a Purple decoding machine was sent to Pearl Harbor although three were sent to London. There was such an overpowering mass of evidence that the Japanese would attack, if at all, at the Philippines or in the South Pacific that Pearl Harbor was disregarded. No warnings of imminent war were sent to the commanders there, and what were later represented as warnings by defenders of Roosevelt actually made General Short and Admiral Kimmel feel all the more certain that there would be no attack on Pearl Harbor.

Roosevelt waited impatiently for the attack in the Far East. He felt that he had to have a Japanese attack to meet the assurances of the 1940 Democratic platform and to avoid having to live up to his agreement in April 1941 to go to war if the Japanese moved too far south, even though they did not attack the American forces. It was for this reason that Roosevelt brushed aside Stimson's proposal that American planes based in the Phillipines attack a Japanese task force moving south and thus start the war. As a stratagem to induce the urgent and indispensable Japanese attack, on December 1 Roosevelt ordered that three small ships be fitted out in the Phillipines, flying the American flag, and be sent out in the path of Japanese task forces to draw the Japanese fire. The first one sent out was the "Isabel," the private yacht of Admiral Thomas C. Hart, commander of the American fleet in the Far East. The Japanese recognized it and refused to be trapped into firing on it. Before the next one in order could be prepared to move, news came of the attack on Pearl Harbor. Recently divulged information reveals the fact that by December 3, Roosevelt was beginning to despair of a Japanese attack and was telling Secretary Henry Morgenthau that he and Churchill would apparently have to decide where and when the United States and Britain would launch their attack on Japan.

By the next morning—the fourth—Roosevelt obtained the welcome news, apparently from the British, that the Japanese were not only going to attack but would make their attack on Pearl Harbor. He did not, as was thought by revisionists for some years, directly or openly order Washington officials not to send any warnings to General Short and Admiral Kimmel at Pearl Harbor. He was too devious and adroit for that. Instead, he only revealed this information to General Marshall and gave an order that all information sent to Pearl Harbor had to be cleared with Marshall. When, about 1:30 on the afternoon of the sixth, the Japanese pilot message forecast the arrival of the Japanese reply to Hull's ultimatum and probable war in a matter of hours, Roosevelt ordered Marshall to disappear until it would be too late effectively to warn Short and Kimmel. This he did, and, according to official testimony, did not get to his office on the seventh until an hour and a half before the time set for the delivery of the Japanese reply to Hull in person and for the attack on Pearl Harbor. Marshall did not even make effective use of the brief time available. He leisurely formulated an ambiguous and inadequate warning, and sent it casually by a slow method. It was not delivered to Short until hours after the Japanese planes had returned to their carriers and the pride of the Pacific battleship fleet had been sunk or disabled.

It would have been a far more mortal disaster had it not been for the fact that the commander of the Japanese task force, Admiral Chuichi Nagumo, was a hesitant and timorous person who had not favored the attack plan, but had had to be placed in command because of seniority rules in the Japanese navy. A bold and resolute commander could have easily returned the next day, destroyed what remained of the navy and, far more important, the machine shops and supply depots, which would have set the United States back at least a year in prosecuting the war in the Pacific. Indeed, the Hawaiian Islands could have been occupied and an American victory indefinitely postponed. In retrospect, the greatest American luck in connection with the Pearl Harbor attack was Admiral Nagumo.

In one of his most stupid moves, and from an assumed strict sense of honor, Hitler, as a member of the Rome-Berlin-Tokyo Axis, declared war on the United States and this enabled Roosevelt to move at once into the European field. A feigned sense of shock over a sneak attack and condolences to the United States for its Pearl Harbor losses sent by Hitler would have created infinite embarassment and problems for Roosevelt and Churchill, but such adroitness would have required a Halifax, Churchill, Roosevelt, or Stalin. Perhaps in estimating Roosevelt's greatest stroke of luck in getting his war, along with a united country, Hitler would have to be ranked next to Nagumo.

Some leading reasons for the historical blackout in relation to revisionism and the Second World War

Despite this voluminous revisionist literature which has appeared since 1945 and its sensational content, there is still virtually no public knowledge of revisionist facts over twenty years after V-J Day. The "man on the street" is just as prone to accept Roosevelt's "day of infamy" legend today as he was on December 8, 1941. A member of the state historical department of a leading eastern state recently wrote me that he had never heard of any revisionist movement relative to the Second World War until he read my article in the Spring 1958 issue of *Modern Age.* By 1928 most literate Americans had a passable knowledge of the facts about the coming of war in 1914 and the American entry in 1917. What are the reasons for the strange contrast in the progress of realistic knowledge after 1918 and after 1945? Since we have already indicated the factors that have all but paralyzed revisionism in Europe since 1945, our examination of the reasons for the blockage of knowledge will be limited to the United States and the so-called historical blackout.

A main reason why revisionism has made little headway since 1945 in attracting public attention in the United States is that the country never really had time to cool off after the war. We have pointed out above that while the emotional situation was not as acute here after 1945 as in Europe and Japan, it was far more tense than it was in the United States in the 1920s. Even as early as the congressional campaign and election of 1918, there was a rift in the wartime political monolith. By the campaign of 1920, disillusionment with the war had set in, and a trend toward isolation from European quarrels had begun to assert itself. The United States refused to sign the Treaty of Versailles or to enter the League of Nations. There was a cooling-off period for about twenty years after 1918. As late as 1941 the overwhelming majority of the American people wished to remain aloof from the European war, and Roosevelt had great difficulty in forcing through a peacetime draft law and in getting any repeal of the neutrality legislation.

Nothing like this happened following 1945. By March 1946 Winston Churchill was proclaiming the cold war in his speech at Fulton, Missouri, delivered with the benediction of President Truman, and a year later Truman actually launched the cold war. This led in 1950 to the outbreak of a hot war in Korea. The Orwellian technique of basing political tenure and bogus economic prosperity on cold and phony warfare had taken over by 1950, to enjoy an indefinite domination over the public mind and political policy. A hot war spontaneously provides plenty of genuine, even if dangerous and misguided, emotion, but a cold war has to be built up almost entirely by propaganda and mythology and sustained on synthethic excitement which is provided by planned propaganda.

The tortures of "Nineteen Eighty-Four," as administered by the "Ministry of Love," have not as yet proved necessary in the United States. The American public proved more susceptible to simple brainwashing through propaganda than Orwell could imagine, although he was himself a veteran propagandist on the BBC. Orwellian doublethinking enabled the Truman, Eisenhower, and Kennedy administrations to formulate and enforce mutually contradictory policies, and the "crimestop" technique of the Orwellian semantic system prevents the public, and many of its leaders, from thinking through any sound program or rational solution. A national policy of perpetual war for perpetual peace does not appear unreasonable or illogical to the American public or its political leaders although it is plainly identical with the cornerstone of the Orwellian system to the effect that "war is peace," and vice versa. Thus far, the propaganda carried on by our "Ministry of Truth," with the almost unanimous aid of our press and other agencies of communication, has been sufficient to maintain popular support of the cold war and our alleged devotion to defending the "free nations" from the menace of communism, the "free nations" apparently including even overt totalitarian regimes if friendly to the United States.

It is obvious that such a brainwashed public is not likely to concern itself seriously with facts and writings that are designed to discredit warfare and furnish a solid basis for substantial peace. It would be about like expecting desert sheiks to concentrate on books devoted to water polo or outboard motorboat racing. The public mind has become all but impenetrable on such matters. In the mid-1920s, for the Allies to deride Uncle Sam as "Uncle Shylock" relative to a paltry twelve billion dollars of war debts made Americans so angry that they were willing to listen to revisionist conclusions. By the mid-1950s, even such flagrantly offensive and ungrateful gestures as "Yanks Go Home," after the United States had poured tens of thousands of lives and over sixty-five billion dollars of foreign aid into lands across the sea, did not even register here. The Washington administrations demanded larger foreign aid appropriations and the public appeared to approve. Congressmen like John Taber, who for years had sought to kill as many appropriations as possible which were devoted to the effort to create a better life here at home, proclaimed that foreign aid was so important that it transcended all considerations of restraint, thrift, and economy which they had so long demanded of appropriations to be used within our own borders. Revisionist views were totally ignored in public policy.

Another explanation of the antipathy or indifference of the public to revisionism since 1945 is to be found in the sharply contrasting intellectual atmosphere of the 1920s and of the period since 1945. Conditions in the 1920s and early 1930s were the most conducive to independent and fearless thought of any decade in modern American history. This was the period of Mencken and Nathan, of the height of the popularity of H. G. Wells. It was an era when James Harvey Robinson's *Mind in the Making* could become a best seller, and Thorstein Veblen was one of the most respected American economists. After 1945, we ran into a period of intellectural conformity perhaps unsurpassed since the supreme power and unity of the Catholic church at the height of the Middle Ages. Between the pressures exerted by the military aspects of the Orwellian cold-war system and those which were equally powerful in the civilian or commercial world, intellectual individuality and independence all but disappeared.

In this era of *Nineteen Eighty-Four, The Organization Man, The Man in the Grey Flannel Suit,* the *Hidden Persuaders,* and *Madison Avenue,* even the average American college graduate became little more inclined to independent thinking than was a

Catholic peasant during the papacy of Innocent III. As Irving Howell pointed out in the *Atlantic* of November 1965, American higher education conformed to the Orwellian cold war system about as conveniently as the Pentagon or American business. When, in the mid-1960s, a small minority of students began to show signs of restlessness, this caused widespread surprise and alarm, and public leaders like Senator Thomas J. Dodd of Connecticut suggested procedure which would have won them kudos from Hitler.

Another reason for the unprecedented resistance to revisionism after the Second World War is the fact that most liberals and radicals, who became the shocktroops and spearhead of revisionism in the 1920s, have since 1945 been overwhelmingly among the chief opponents of any acceptance of revisionist facts and conclusions. They were the leaders of the war party in Britain, France, and the United States for months or years before 1939 and 1941, and they have never recanted. Although most of the prominent liberals heartily supported Wilson's war after 1917, they were completely disillusioned by the "peace" treaty and led the revisionist parade after 1919. Especially notable were Herbert Croly and his editorial associates on the *New Republic.* They recanted, but plenty. Oswald Garrison Villard and most of his associates on the *Nation* did not need to recant, for they had never supported American intervention in 1917 with any enthusiasm.

A leading reason why the liberals and radicals have been unable to revise their prewar views and attitudes is that their hatred of Hitler and Mussolini has been just too great to permit them to accept any facts, however well established, that might to any degree diminish the guilt with which these men were charged from 1939 onward—or from 1935, for that matter. The American liberals introduced the dangerous doctrine that we must do battle with any foreign country whose political ideology and practices do not accord with liberal beliefs and prejudices. This opens the door to perpetual war—a state of "permanent war," as *Time* expressed it, since we shall never run out of foreign nations whose public opinions and operations do not charm American liberals or any other powerful war-minded groups in the country. In such a case, "facts can be damned." There was no comparable prewar liberal hatred of Stalin to have to live down despite the brutal and scandalous Soviet trials of the mid-1930s. The hatred of Hitler has been especially bitter among some minority groups that were notably enthusiastic about the revisionism that followed the First World War.

Indeed, the hesitancy in setting down any historical facts that might present the diplomacy of Hitler and Mussolini in any more favorable light than that of wartime appears to have extended to many revisionists of today, even to those of a conservative temperament. After the First World War, most of the American revisionist historical writing was on the European background of August 1914. There were only four important and explicitly revisionist books written on the American entry into the war—those by Tansill, Grattan, Millis and J. K. Turner—while there were a dozen or more on the European situation published in Europe and the United States. The first definitive book on American entry, Tansill's *America Goes to War,* did not appear until 1938, ten years after Fay's *Origins of the World War.*

After the Second World War, the revisionist books written by American authors have dealt chiefly with American entry into the war. There has not been a revisionist book or an extended and thorough revisionist article which sets forth the truth about 1939 that has been written by an American author and published here. The nearest approach is the able and informed treatment of the European background in Tansill's classic *Back Door to War,* but this book is devoted primarily to the American entry into the war. Either aversion to even the slightest mitigation of the wartime indictment of Hitler and Mussolini, or fear of the results, appears to have prevented most revisionists in both the United States and Europe from having systematically tackled the crisis of 1939 in over twenty-five years after the events. A. J. P. Taylor's above-mentioned *Origins of the Second World War,* by an English historian, was the first to do so, and it has not stimulated others to emulate this precedent since 1961.

The anti-interventionist groups of 1937 and thereafter, like America First, were primarily conservative and for the most part welcomed the early revisionist publications. But they soon fell in line with the cold war because of the business advantages in industry, trade, and finance which an extravagant armament program and foreign aid provided. Thereafter, they feared or refused to give any open support, financial or otherwise, to a scholarly movement which undermined the cold war assumptions as thoroughly as it did the interventionist mythology of 1939–1941. Hence, revisionism since 1947 has not only been unpopular or ignored but also poverty-stricken. On the other hand, the rich foundations have given lavish aid to the writing of antirevisionist books. About $150,000 was given to aid the publication of the Langer and Gleason volumes, the most impressive effort to whitewash the diplomatic record of Roosevelt and Churchill, and Roberta Wohlstetter was generously subsidized to produce her book on Pearl Harbor which attempted to blur out the revisionist conclusions relative to the Japanese attack and the failure to warn the Pearl Harbor commanders.

Other factors have led to the almost incredible obstruction of revisionism since 1945. The excessive "security" policies and measures which have been adopted under the cold-war system have greatly increased fear and timidity on the part of public officials, scholars, and the general public. Since revisionism implicitly and logically challenged the whole fabric of American public policy, especially foreign policy, after Pearl Harbor, it has been precarious to espouse it. It has become hazardous to work for peace except through war. The press and all other agencies of communications, naturally, prefer the emotion-provoking frame of reference of a cold war to the prosaic scholarship of revisionism. In the 1920s, the press was congenial to revisionism because it buttressed our prevailing public policies relative to reparations, war debts, isolationism, disarmament, neutrality and the like. Today, revisionism challenges the honesty, intelligence, and integrity of our basic foreign policies by its devastating revelation of the disastrous results of our martial world-meddling since 1937, while our communications agencies, for the most part, applaud and warmly support our militant interventionist foreign policy.

Outstanding publication and promotional difficulties with respect to revisionism and the Second World War

Especially important is the difficulty in having revisionist books published under auspices likely to arouse extensive public interest and in getting them presented to the reading public honestly and effectively. There have only been two publishers, and these relatively small ones, which have consistently published revisionist books: the Henry Regnery Company in Chicago and the Devin-

Adair Company in New York City. Only six other small publishers have produced a revisionist book—one book only in each of these cases save for the Yale University Press, which brought out both of Beard's volumes because the director was a close friend and great admirer of Beard, and the Rutgers University Press. University presses have found it precarious to indulge in revisionist publication; W. T. Couch, the able head of the University of Chicago Press, was dismissed primarily because he published so peripheral a revisionist volume as A. Frank Reel's admirable book, *The Case of General Yamashita.* The Rutgers University Press has shown the greatest courage in this matter by publishing Richard N. Current's *Secretary Stimson,* Anne Armstrong's *Unconditional Surrender,* and Nicholas Balabkins's *Germany Under Direct Controls.*

Not one large commercial publisher in the United States has brought out a single substantial and literal revisionist book since Pearl Harbor.* This stands out in sharp contrast to the attitude of publishers toward revisionist volumes in the 1920s and the 1930s. The largest publishers were then very eager to get such books. Professor Fay's classic work was published by the Macmillan Company, and the monumental two-volume work of John S. Ewart by Doran. Alfred Knopf published my *Genesis* and a veritable library of revisionist books in the 1920s, but in 1953 he refused even to consider so mild and restrained a revisionist book as Professor Current's scholarly study of the public career of Secretary Henry L. Stimson.

There are a number of obvious reasons why the large publishers shy away from revisionist books today. In the first place, they are American citizens and, for reasons already discussed, like most of their fellow Americans, they dislike giving up their prewar and wartime convictions, emotions, hatreds, and prejudices; most of them just do not like revisionists and revisionism. Further, knowing that revisionism is publicly unpopular, they realize that revisionist books are not likely to sell well; hence, revisionist publication is relatively poor business. Moreover, those publishers who may privately espouse revisionism and would like to see some

---

*The nearest approach was the publication of the prison memoirs of Shigenori Togo, the wartime foreign minister of Japan, *The Cause of Japan,* by Simon and Schuster, in September 1956.

revisionist books published, even if they had to do it with slight profit or even a small loss, just cannot consider a revisionist book on its own merits or by itself alone. They have to take into account its possible reaction on the general publishing trade and the book-buying public. The loss that they could sustain through merely publishing a revisionist volume might be nothing as compared to what they would lose by the unfortunate impression such publication might make or from the retaliation which might follow.

They are especially alarmed at the possible retaliation at the hands of the various book clubs, since all the powerful ones are tightly controlled by those groups and interests most hostile to revisionism today. William Henry Chamberlin's *America's Second Crusade* is the one revisionist treatment of the Second World War which is admirably suited for popular sale and reading. It is precisely comparable to Walter Millis's *Road to War* on our entry into the First World War. The Millis book was a Book-of-the-Month–Club selection and sold by the hundreds of thousands. The head of one of the largest publishing houses in the world knew and liked Chamberlin, admired his book, and personally would have liked to publish it. But he held, quite understandably, that he did not feel that he could do so in the light of his responsibilities to his stockholders. As he put it, if he published the Chamberlin book, his company probably would not get another Book-of-the-Month–Club adoption in a decade. The Chamberlin book was published by Henry Regnery.

A comparison of its fate with that of the Millis *Road to War* is instructive. Macy's in New York City ordered fifty copies of the Chamberlin book and returned forty as "unsold." If it could have been handled on its merits, surely five or six thousand copies would have been sold. A year after the date of publication, there was still not a copy of the book in the New York Public Library or any of its branches. Revisionist books are virtually boycotted, so far as sales to the general run of public libraries are concerned. The woman who is said to exert a greater influence upon book orders by libraries than any other person in the United States is vehemently antirevisionist. So far as possible she sees to it that revisionist books are either ignored or smeared in her advice to librarians seeking guidance as to purchases. She also possesses considerable influence on purchases by book stores.

Even when revisionist books get into stores, clerks frequently refuse to display them and, in some cases, even lie about their availability. In the book department of America's outstanding store, a woman sought to purchase a copy of what was then the most widely read revisionist book. The clerk told her decisively that the supply was exhausted and no copies were available. The customer suspected that she was lying and was able to get the head of the store, who happened to have revisionist sympathies, to make an investigation. It was found that over fifty copies were hidden under the counter and that the clerk had known that this was the case. The head of the store was so outraged that he ordered the book department to make a special display of the hitherto concealed book.

The leading magazines are just as reluctant to publish revisionist articles as the large commercial publishers are to publish any revisionist books. This also stands out in complete contrast to the situation in the 1920s, when the editors of the better periodicals were eager to get authoritative articles by leading revisionists. All of the many articles I wrote on revisionism in the 1920s and early 1930s were solicited by the editors. So far as I know, this was true of other revisionist writers. But not a substantial revisionist article has been printed in a popular and powerful American periodical since Pearl Harbor. At the same time, American periodicals are open to all manner of antirevisionist contributions, and in recent years have published a great mass of the most virulent Germanophobia which is probably the chief obstacle to scholarly revisionism today. When American Germanophobes are not regarded as adequate to the task, they seek out European vitriol-vendors like Hugh Trevor-Roper. The reasons for editorial allergy to revisionist articles are the same as those that affect the heads of the large commmercial publishing houses relative to revisionist books.

Incredible as it may seem, not only publishers but even printers have sought to suppress revisionist material. When I presented a restrained brochure, based on extensive research and designed to set forth the basic facts about the military and political career of Marshal Pétain, to a printing firm in New York City, the printers refused to put the material into type unless it was approved by the censorship department of one of the most powerful and vehemently antirevisionist minority groups in the country. Whereupon, I took the copy to a leading upstate New York printing firm which was not accessible to this form of pressure. The episode reminded one of the prepublication censorship which existed back in the days of Copernicus. There have also been attempts to suppress even the most factual revisionist material. A leading minority antirevisionist organization sought to prevent further distribution of *A Select Bibliography of Revisionist Books* that I had prepared with the aid of several able revisionist historians. The publisher was something less than sympathetic with this effort, and the would-be censor retreated in some dismay.

The handicaps imposed on revisionist books are not limited to the difficulties of publication and distribution. When these books are published, they have usually been ignored, obscured or smeared. They have rarely been given decent notice or honest reviews, even if the opinion of the reviewer might be unfavorable. As one of the leading blackout organizations has advised its agents, it is preferable to ignore a book entirely if one wishes to assure killing its distribution and influence. Even a viciously unfair review will at least call attention to the volume and may arouse some curiosity and interest. To ignore it completely will do more than anything else to consign it to oblivion. Under the editorship of Guy Stanton Ford, it was the announced policy of the *American Historical Review* not to review "controversial" volumes but, upon careful examination, it turned out that "controversial" meant "revisionist." Highly controversial antirevisionist books in the field were given a good position and reviews as long as those usually accorded to other books of comparable importance.

When revisionist books are actually listed and reviewed, they are usually given an obscure position, often being put in the book notes. This was the case with Dr. Luigi Villari's book on *Italian Foreign Policy Under Mussolini.* Although it was a book of major importance in diplomatic history—the only authoritative volume which had appeared on the subject—and the author was the most distinguished living authority in the field, the book was consigned to the book note section of the *American Historical Review,* and outrageously smeared. It should be pointed out, in fairness, however, that for a time after Dr. Boyd C. Shafer succeeded Dr. Ford as editor, revisionist books were given a somewhat more decent treatment in the *American Historical Review.* Space limitations do not permit me to cite here in detail the fate of the leading revisionist books at the hands of scholarly periodicals and the book review sections of leading periodicals and newspapers. Most of them have their permanent cabal of antirevisionist and Germanophobic reviewers. I have gone into this matter at length in the first chapter of *Perpetual War for Perpetual Peace.*

The essence of the situation is that no matter how many revisionist books are produced, how high their quality, or how sensational their revelations, they will have no effect on the American public until this public learns of the existence, nature, and importance of revisionist literature. That they have not been able to do so as yet is obvious, and the obstacles that have thus far proved effective have not been reduced to any noticeable extent. Indeed, a more malicious and misleading obstacle has arisen in the tidal wave of Germanophobia with which our journalism and all other communication agencies have been drenched since the time of the Eichmann trial in 1961, a matter to which Professor Connors devotes some trenchant pages later on.

Official aspects of the historical blackout

Thus far, I have dealt mainly with private or non-official efforts to obscure the truth relative to the causes and results of the Second World War. The official censorship has been as unrelenting and in many ways more shocking. Those who publish official documents do not have to be restrained by considerations of profit and loss. More than a decade ago, Charles Austin Beard blasted the procedure of the State Department in its tendency to permit historians favorable to the official foreign policy to use the public documents rather freely, while denying such access to anybody suspected of revisionist sympathies. This led to some momentary relaxation of censorship, and it was fortunate that Professor Tansill was able to carry on much of his research at this time. But soon the censorship, restrictions, and favoritism returned full force. As an example of the continuing favoritism it is interesting to note that in preparing their books on the career of the late President Kennedy, Theodore C. Sorensen and Arthur M. Schlesinger, Jr., were given access to top-secret documents such as the Vienna conference transcript which outsiders are not likely to see until after 1984.

The Republicans promised drastic reform of this abuse when they came into power in 1953, but they failed to implement these assurances and, under Secretary Dulles, the scandal grew to far greater proportions than under Democratic auspices. The same historical adviser, Dr. G. Bernard Noble, was continued in the service and actually promoted to be director of the historical division of the State Department. He was a Democrat, a Rhodes scholar, and known to be one of the most frenzied advocates of our intervention in the Second World War among all American social scientists and an implacable enemy of revisionism.

In May 1953 the State Department promised that all records of the international conferences during the Second World War would be ready for publication within a year and that all other documents on the period since 1930 would be speedily published.

Nothing was done until the spring of 1955, when the documents on the Yalta conference were finally published. It was evident, and soon proved, that these had been garbled and censored in flagrant fashion. Two able members of the historical staff of the department, Dr. Bryton Barron and Dr. Donald Dozer, protested against this suppression and distortion of documents. Noble forced Barron into premature retirement without pay and discharged Dozer. The latter was reinstated by the Civil Service Commission, but Noble was able to get him discharged again— and this time permanently. Barron had been assigned to compile the material bearing on the Yalta conference, and Dozer that on the Cairo-Teheran conferences. When the Teheran documents were published, Dozer examined them carefully and found that they had been as badly manhandled by selection and distortion as the Yalta documents had been.

In the meantime, some thirty-seven volumes dealing with our foreign policy since 1939 were collected and made ready for publication. But nothing was sent to the printer and, in the spring of 1958, the State Department blandly announced that it did not propose to publish any of these volumes in the predictable future. It gave as the reason the assertion that publication might possibly offend some persons among our NATO allies. To give this amazing procedure some semblance of historical authority, a handpicked committee was appointed in 1957 to advise the department on publication. The personnel of the committee, which did not contain one revisionist historian, assured that the right advice would be turned in. The chairman was none other than Professor Dexter Perkins, admittedly a jolly and affable historical politician, but also one of the half-dozen outstanding and unremitting opponents of revisionist scholarship in this country. The committee dutifully reported that publication of any of the thirty-seven volumes would not be politically expedient. After the inauguration of President Kennedy, increased interest and activity ensued and by the end of 1964 some eighteen volumes had been published covering the years 1940 through 1943, thus still leaving a twenty-year gap. Not all the blame can be assigned to the State Department since some congressmen have resisted paying over the necessary funds.

When Dr. Barron appeared before a senatorial committee to protest against the censorship and delays, he was allowed only eleven minutes to testify, although witnesses supporting the official censorship were allowed ample time. As one of the abler editorial writers in the country commented, quite correctly: "Such a record of concealment and duplicity is unparalleled. Its only counterpart is the 'memory hole' in George Orwell's *Nineteen Eighty-Four,* where an authoritarian regime of the future was depicted as disposing of all documents and facts that failed to fit into the current party line." All this is hardly consistent with the assumed role of the United States as the leader of the "free nations" or with our bitter condemnation of the Russians for censoring their official documents.

When the documents on the Yalta, Teheran, and Potsdam conferences were published, Professor Norman Graebner of the University of Illinois declared in the July 1962 issue of the *American Historical Review* that "the editors have eliminated nothing of significance from the official record. Their care and thoughtfulness in preparing these publications are apparent everywhere." And in the same issue of this scholarly periodical it was announced that the advisory committee representing the American Historical Association, Dexter Perkins, Fred H. Harrington, and Richard W. Leopold, "expressed its deep appreciation of the scholarly work and achievements of the chief of the historical division, Bernard Noble."

There are, of course, some vital official documents dealing with the onset of the Second World War that our government has never dreamed of publishing at any time and are so full of dynamite that not even historians engaged in whitewashing the official record are allowed to make any practical use of them. Such are the so-called Kent Documents, namely, the nearly two thousand secret messages illegally exchanged in the American code between Churchill and Roosevelt from September 1939 onward. Churchill himself has frankly told us that these documents contain most of the really vital facts about the collaboration between him and Roosevelt in their joint efforts to bring the United States into the war. Their explosive content can well be discerned from the fact that when the most impressive historical effort to whitewash the Roosevelt-Churchill record was about to be undertaken, Churchill threatened the principal author with a court suit if he made use of these Kent Documents.

The origin, nature, and implications of the Kent Documents are best described in pages 310–320 of Richard J. Whalen's biography of Joseph P. Kennedy, *The Founding Father* (1964); and in an article on that subject by Whalen in the magazine *Diplomat,* November 1965. In his article, "The Strange Case of Tyler Kent," Whalen states that Langer and Gleason did not even know of the existence of the Kent Documents until Churchill mentioned them in his postwar memoirs. He based this statement on a letter just received from Langer which said: "Until Churchill spoke of these messages, there was no reason to even suspect they existed."

This is obviously preposterous. Even an alert reader of the newspapers and magazines of the first half of the 1940s could hardly have failed to have seen references to the existence of the Kent Documents and their general nature. It is not likely that Langer, with his special interest in diplomatic history and his high position in the Office of Strategic Services, would have been more ignorant than the average literate "man in the street." Moreover, it was a former student of Langer who informed me that Langer told him that Churchill had threatened him with a court suit if he made use of the Kent Documents. Without raising the issue of the relative veracity of Langer and his student and protégé, one can safely say that Langer's statement that he did not know of the existence of the Kent Documents until he read about them in the Churchill memoirs passes the limit of credibility. I discussed this with a leading professor of modern European history since the Whalen article appeared. He said that surely by 1944 he had a considerable dossier on the Kent case collected from published accounts. He doubted if his experience was unusual. John Howland Snow's *Case of Tyler Kent,* the best treatment of the case prior to that by Whalen, appeared in 1946. Churchill's *Gathering Storm* was not published until 1949, and *Their Finest Hour* not until 1950.

One interesting byproduct of Whalen's researches was the discovery that Stalin surely had the Kent Documents in his possession during the wartime conferences. Stalin may very well have used their knowledge of this fact to blackmail Roosevelt and Churchill into making extensive concessions to Russia, especially at Teheran and Yalta, and possibly to pressure Truman into certifying them at Potsdam. Whalen states that such a thesis is "farfetched." Actually, the American intelligence experts whom I induced to help Whalen on this matter of the codes of 1940–41 made it clear that the intelligence personnel of any of the main European countries could read, and probably were reading, the Gray code in which the Kent Documents were sent, so far as they *were* in code. Moreover, a leading American businessman told me personally in the spring of 1946 that in 1945 he had purchased a microfilm of the Kent Documents from Russian sources and had sent it to Truman.

It may be granted that it is only a possibility that Stalin used these documents for the purpose of diplomatic blackmail, but he surely had them if he wished to use them for this purpose. He may not have needed to do so anyway, because when Russia had driven the Germans out of eastern Europe, Churchill and Roosevelt faced the bald fact that they would probably have to write off this area or start World War III.

The suppression of documents relative to responsibility for the Second World War extends, of course, far beyond all Anglo-American activities and relations. When the Communists and Socialists in Russia, Germany, and Austria published their archives following 1918 in order to discredit the old imperial regimes, this forced the British and French ultimately to follow suit to a limited extent. Eventually, scholars had most of the documentary material at their disposal. But neither the British nor the French published all of their documents. It was interesting to find Bernadotte Schmitt, perhaps the outstanding Anglomaniac among American historians, heading a list of international scholars protesting in the London *Times* of September 18, 1965, against the

British failure to open all of their archives bearing on the First World War over fifty years after 1914.

Nothing like this publication of documents after 1918 was possible after the Second World War. The victorious Allied powers, chiefly Britain and the United States, captured the German and Italian archives, except for some of the more vital Italian materials which the Italian Communists destroyed, with Allied connivance and encouragement, when they captured and murdered Mussolini. Hence, West Germany and Italy could not have published all their documents after 1945, even if they wished to do so, for they did not possess them. The Bonn government has now received the substance of the captured German documents, and many of those taken from Italy have been returned. The United States has kept a full microfilm copy of all returned documents.

The Germans and Italians cannot be expected to publish much that is likely to modify the wartime indictment of Hitler and Mussolini. One of the main obstacles to the development and acceptance of revisionism in regard to the Second World War is the curious but bitter opposition of the Bonn government in West Germany to revisionist publications on the causes of the Second World War that would place Germany in a better light by bringing out the truth on 1939. This attitude stands in marked contrast with the situation under the Weimar Republic in the 1920s when the government officials took the lead in publishing the documents on the background of the First World War, warmly and directly encouraged revisionist writings, sometimes subsidizing them, and went out of their way to honor foreign scholars who came to Germany to lecture on the subject.

The publication of forthright revisionist material on the Second World War by West Germans was made a public crime although this order was not always rigorously enforced. The Bonn regime has its coterie of court historians who denounce revisionism as heatedly as those in Britain, France, or the United States. When the Bonn government recently regained possession of the German documents which the Allies had seized, these were censored to a considerable extent and restrictions placed on their use, much as had been done previously in the case of the American archives. A scholarly friend of mine recently had to check on a document in the archives in Arlington, Virginia, for a German friend who found it too difficult to get at it in Bonn. This strange situation has been brought on by the fear that the facts about the causes of war in 1939 may encourage a revival of pro-Hitler sentiment in Germany, and because of American pressure on West Germany relative to World War II reparations.

The postwar Italian government has also been hostile to revisionist publications, although some Italian authors have defied government displeasure, notably Dr. Luigi Villari and Messrs. Tomaro, Anfuso, and D'Aroma, but Villari had to get his important books published in the United States and the other authors mentioned above deal chiefly with internal Italian affairs. Indeed, Dr. Villari wrote me that, much as he would like to do so, he would have great difficulty in getting an Italian translation of my 1958 *Liberation* article published in Italy. There has not, however, been any such avalanche of vilification of Mussolini in Italy as there has been of Hitler in Germany. In fact, there has recently been some indication of a revived Italian appreciation of the benefits that Mussolini's achievements brought to Italy.

Although the Russians have not published any such revolutionary revisionist material as was the case after the First World War, they have made some start in publishing the Russian documents. In 1957 they published a two-volume collection of the correspondence of Stalin with Roosevelt and Churchill during the war. In 1961 they published a collection of documents on the Teheran conference, limited to the discussions between Stalin, Roosevelt, and Churchill. In 1965 they published documents on the Yalta conference and promised to follow with those on the Potsdam conference. A preliminary checking of the Russian documents published thus far indicates that the translations are accurate and the documents, so far as published, are reliable.

The main import of official censorship is that the striking revisionist verdict relative to responsibility for the Second World War is probably less drastic than it will be if and when all the documents are available. If the documents now suppressed would lessen the already severe indictment of the Allied wartime leaders, elementary logic and strategy support the assumption that they would have been published long before the present moment in order to modify or eliminate the severe judgments already set forth in existing revisionist volumes.

One paradox should be noted relative to the status and results of revisionism after the two World Wars. After the First World

War, the revisionist verdict as to the responsibility for the war was very generally accepted by scholars and intelligent public leaders, but little was done about it in the way of revising the European postwar system that had been based on the lies and propaganda of wartime. If the logical steps had been taken to revise the postwar treaties while the Weimar Republic was in existence, it is unlikely that Hitler would ever have risen to power in Germany, that there would have been any Second World War, or that any cold war would have come on its heels. After the Second World War, while the facts brought forth by revisionism as to the responsibility for the war have been ignored, indeed, are virtually unknown to the publics among the victorious Allies, there has been an almost complete revision of American public policy toward our former enemies. Both West Germany and, to a lesser extent, Japan have been almost forcibly rearmed and given extensive material aid so that they can now function as allies against our former ally, Soviet Russia. One can imagine the outcry if, say, in 1925, we had insisted that Germany and Austria must rearm to the hilt and we had expressed our determination to enable them to do so.

Any such situation as has taken place since 1945 can only be possible in an era of Orwellian double-thinking and "crimestop." We spent about $400 billion to destroy the military power of Germany and Japan and, after its destruction, we have poured in more billions to restore their military facilities. If it were conceivable that we could fight a third world war without exterminating all the participants, we might envisage a situation where, after destroying Russian power, we proceeded to give her billions to rebuild her fighting forces to defend us against China and India.

One lesson that revisionism might teach us is that we should learn from its publications attitudes and facts which could protect us against repeated folly and tragedy. The eminent philosopher, John Dewey, told a friend of mine that if he had not been so wrong in his attitude toward the First World War (as exemplified by his *German Philosophy and Politics*), he might have succumbed to the propaganda that led us into the Second World War. But publics appear to profit less by experience than pragmatic philosophers. They seem to vindicate Hegel's classic observation that the only lesson that history teaches us is that we learn nothing from history. In an age of hydrogen bombs, intercontinental guided missiles, terrifyingly lethal chemical and bacterial warfare, and pushbutton military technology, we shall have to do better than the publics of Hegel's time if we are to have any prospect of survival or of attaining such a degree of peace, security, and well-being as would justify survival. But the American public can hardly learn any lesson from revisionism if it does not even know that it exists, to say nothing of its content and implications.

Unless and until we can break through the historical blackout, now supported even by public policy, and enable the peoples of the world to know the facts concerning international relations during the last four decades, including the South Vietnam War, there can be no real hope for the peace, security, and prosperity which the present triumphs of science and technology could make possible.

Historical and Educational Losses Due to the Historical Blackout, and the Significance of A. J. P. Taylor's *Origins of the Second World War*

A lost generation in historical writing and teaching

Those who are now coming to maturity are greatly handicapped in regard to historical information and realism as compared to my own generation. As has been noted, the 1920s and early 1930s were an era of iconoclasm and debunking, well symbolized by Mencken and Nathan and the *American Mercury*. It was difficult in those days to maintain an intellectual blackout anywhere, even in the realm of historical writing. My first ardent attack on any form of historical blackout appeared in the first number of the *Mercury* at Mencken's suggestion, even insistence. The iconoclastic trend in history took the form of what has come to be known as revisionism, which was devoted to wiping out the vestiges of the wartime propaganda of the previous decade.

The generation which was born or has been educated since 1936 or thereabouts is, historically speaking, a lost generation—a group of youthful Rip van Winkles. By 1937 the majority of American liberal intellectuals were adopting the internationalist ideology of the popular front based on the "collective security" formula which Litvinov had so successfully propagated at Geneva. Nearly all liberals, and a surprising number of conservatives, jumped on the interventionist and anti-German bandwagon then being chartered and steered by President Roosevelt and Harry Hopkins. The majority of American historians belonged to the liberal camp and became ardent interventionists.

From this time onward, most history teaching and writing in this country, in dealing with recent world events, increasingly took on the form of a fanciful, and in part unconsciously malicious fairytale. It presented the pattern of the late 1930s and the 1940s as a planetary crusading arena in which a triumvirate of St. Georges—Franklin D. Roosevelt, Winston Churchill, and Joseph Stalin—were bravely united in a holy war to slay the Nazi dragon. Even before Hitler had shot himself in a Berlin bunker, Roosevelt and Churchill had begun to suspect that perhaps their erstwhile Soviet fellow crusader for freedom, justice, and peace was more of a menace to utopia than the Nazi "madman." In due time, even Stalin's successor in the Kremlin came to be regarded as a threat to the "free world," although he had removed Stalin from the Kremlin display window and buried him like any ordinary mortal.

In the 1920s and early 1930s, the evidence of the mistakes which the United States had made in its first crusade in Europe under the leadership of Woodrow Wilson was frankly brought forth and displayed before the American educational world and reading public. Not so with the far greater blunders of our second global crusade. The disagreeable facts were consigned to the Orwellian "memory hole," and the few books which sought to present the salutary truth were, as has been indicated above, either ignored or unfairly derided. The generation which grew up during this ill-fated crusading era has been thoroughly brainwashed in regard to the historical basis of world affairs and the role of the United States therein. It has passed little if any beyond the intellectual and informational confines of President Roosevelt's colorful but misleading "day of infamy" rhetoric. Richard J. Whalen well summarized the situation in the *National Review* of April 20, 1965: "The tidal wave of disillusionment that swept through the West after World War I brought a flood of scholarly and popular books debunking the official history of the war. Revisionism became an integral part of the dominant liberalism of the period. But the younger journalists and historians who revolted against their elders following World War I have in the years since the last war succeeded brilliantly in forestalling a like revolt against themselves. And so we have missed the debunking generation.''

It has long since been observed that historical truth is the first casualty of a war. American historiography, in dealing with world affairs, was sadly ailing before September 1939 and was mortally ill by Pearl Harbor, in December 1941. The majority of historians ardently supported intervention in the European maelstrom. A surprisingly large group accepted posts involved in the war effort and propaganda, some of them of much prominence and responsibility. Hence, they had a powerful vested interest in preserving and defending the dragon-killing legend.

Most historians were ardently inflamed by the emotions engendered by the wartime propaganda. Many of them, no doubt, were honestly convinced of the soundness of this interventionist and crusading propaganda. Those few who had kept their heads and really knew the score were wise enough to keep their counsel to themselves in order to hold their posts and have some assurance of promotion. Whatever the reasons for the debacle, it is certain that historical standards and products affected by recent world events have declined to a lower level, so far as integrity and objectivity are concerned, than at any period since the close of the Counter-Reformation. For anything comparable in this country one would have to look back to the political tracts of the period of the Civil War and Reconstruction. Indeed, it is no exaggeration to say that those historians who today accept, aid and abet, and promote the extreme Germanophobia of recent years are no more accurate in their approach to national socialist Germany than Orosius was in his description and appraisal of pre-Christian pagan culture.

In the 1920s there was a strong reaction against the military obsession with intervention in foreign quarrels. For more than a decade, a trend towards peace, isolation, and antimilitarism ensued. Historical writing and teaching rather generally adjusted to this climate of intellectual opinion. Revisionism sprang up and, by and large, had won the battle against the bitter-enders of the previous decade by the end of the 1920s. Leading revisionist historians, such as Sidney Bradshaw Fay and Charles Callan Tansill, were lavishly praised by members of their craft. The journalistic culmination of revisionist spirit and lore, Walter Millis's *Road to*

War, became one of the outstanding best sellers of the 1930s.

There was, as has been pointed out earlier, no such extensive cooling-off period or escape from militant emotions after V-J Day in 1945. Along with the perpetuation of propaganda in the guise of history came a powerful effort to prevent those who had some real regard for historical truth from getting their facts and thoughts before the American public. This project has come, as we have seen, to be known as the "historical blackout." It involved a comprehensive effort since the outbreak of the Second World War to suppress the truth relative to the causes and merits of the great conflict that began in 1939 and the manner in which the United States entered it. This has consisted in ignoring or suppressing facts that ran counter to the wartime propaganda when writing books on these subjects, and in suppressing, ignoring, or seeking to discredit those books which have taken account of such facts.

It has often been asserted that this historical blackout is today a sinister and deliberate plot to obstruct the truth and degrade history. This is undoubtedly the truth with respect to the program and activities of some minority groups and ideological organizations which have a special vested interest in perpetuating the wartime mythology. But, for the most part, it has become more the unconscious product of three decades of indoctrination and brainwashing that grew out of interventionist and wartime propaganda. Even most professional historians who began their teaching careers after 1937 have automatically come to accept as truth the distortions of prewar and wartime interventionism. The current blackout is as much an inevitable and automatic reaction to brainwashing as a perverse conspiracy. But this does not make it any less difficult to resist or overcome. As Taylor has pointed out, the conviction of these historians that they are writing unbiased history is all too often self-deception: "The academic historians of the West may assert their scholarly independence even when they are engaged by a government department; but they are as much 'engaged' as though they wore the handsome uniforms designed for German professors by Dr. Goebbels."

This situation following the Second World War is, thus, a complete reversal of what happened after the First World War when revisionism carried the day in the historical forum within a decade after the armistice of November 11, 1918. Even some of the outstanding leaders of revisionism after the First World War, such as Sidney B. Fay and William L. Langer, abandoned World War I revisionism, succumbed to the historical blackout, and gave warm support to the dragon-slaying fantasy. In only a little over a year and a half after the armistice of 1918 Fay had blasted for all time the myth of the unique guilt of a Hohenzollern gorilla, as the kaiser had been portrayed during the conflict. Within a decade after the close of the war, a veritable library of revisionist books had been produced on responsibility for the calamity of 1914.

Despite the fact that the documentary material to support revisionism after the Second World War is more profuse, cogent, and convincing than after 1918, as of today not a single volume by an American scholar devoted exclusively to the causes of the Second World War has been published in the United States—some twenty-six years after the outbreak of the war and twenty years after its close.

To be sure, one book related to the field was published, *Back Door to War,* by Charles Callan Tansill, long dean of American diplomatic historians. It has about as much material on responsibility for 1939 as Professor Taylor's *Origins of the Second World War,* is more thoroughly documented, and arrives at much the same conclusions as Taylor. But the Tansill book was designed primarily to indicate by impressive documentation how, as Clare Booth Luce expressed it, President Roosevelt had lied the United States into war from 1937 to 1941. Hence, there was much more interest in what Tansill had to say about the antecedents of Pearl Harbor than in his treatment of the responsibility for the European war in 1939, and Tansill's extensive and valuable material on the latter subject was generally slighted. There have been a number of important and distinguished books by American writers which have supplemented Tansill's account of American entry into the Second World War but for the most part they have been ignored or smeared, and the dragon-slaying fiction still remains almost immaculate and impregnable.

Professor Tansill's book, *America Goes to War,* which was published in 1938 and is far and away the best account of American entry into war in 1917, was declared by Dr. Henry Steele Commager to be "the most valuable contribution to the history of the prewar years in our literature and one of the most notable achievements of historical scholarship of this generation." His

Back Door to War is an equally learned, scholarly, and erudite account of our entry into the Second World War, but orthodox historians have been inclined to dismiss it as merely superficial and biased counterpropaganda. Even Charles Austin Beard, dean of American historians and political scientists, was ruthlessly smeared for presuming to protect Clio's chastity by two of the best books he ever wrote.

William Henry Chamberlin's *America's Second Crusade,* the only substantial but popular account of our entry into the Second World War, was highly comparable to Millis's *Road to War* on our intervention in 1917. But, whereas Millis's book sold a quarter of a million copies, a year after the Chamberlin book was published there was, as we noted above, not one copy listed in the New York Public Library or in any of its many branches.

It need not be alleged that all those who operate book clubs and book services deliberately aim to pervert or frustrate historical truth relative to world affairs. Some of them presumably regard themselves as supporting historical truth. They just do not know what it is. They are emotionally congenial to the wartime legends, and most historians they know seem to agree with them. Both have been brainwashed for a generation.

The essence of what has preceded is that the generation which has gained its historical knowledge and perspectives since the late 1930s has been deprived, cheated, and handicapped by the distortion and suppression of historical facts relative to world affairs. This is especially unfortunate because of the transcendent role of world relations and policies in the everyday life, interests, decisions, and destiny of the American citizens of today. The handicap is true even if a person has been a history major in college. Indeed, it is likely that he will have been more victimized by historical errors as a result of more copious and intensive indoctrination with historical fiction than one who has specialized in literature, art, or music.

A. J. P. Taylor's Origins of the Second World War: *a new epoch in revisionist historiography*

The importance of Professor Taylor's highly controversial volume lies in the fact that it could prove unusually potent in blasting through the historical blackout. Through a fortunate combination of circumstances, the book has shaken up Britain more than any other historical work in the field of world affairs since the writings of E. D. Morel over forty years ago. It was hoped that the American edition could do as well in producing a flash of light which would penetrate the historical blackout of a generation's duration. For the lost generation, historically speaking, the great value of the Taylor book is that it could be the logical starting-point for them in recovering the all-important lost pages of history, out of which they have been cheated by brainwashing and the historical blackout.

Professor Taylor's book is the first to be published in any language which is exclusively devoted to the task of debunking the dragon-slaying travesty which has colored and distorted historical perspective for over a quarter of a century.

It is probable that no living historian could be more appropriate as an effective and convincing author of such a book. In the first place, he is an English scholar. Due to Rhodes scholarships and other related items which promote Anglophilism in the United States, there is a special aura attaching to English historians, their scholarship, and their implied words of wisdom. This gives Taylor and his book special prestige in this country. Then, he is easily the best known and most popular of contemporary British historians. Further, he is the author of a number of substantial historical works dealing with contemporary history and diplomatic relations, most of them devoted in part at least to recent German history. In other words, he is a specialist in the field covered by his book under consideration here, which is not the case with his bitter critics such as A. L. Rowse and Hugh R. Trevor-Roper, the former a specialist in Tudor history and poetry and the latter in Stuart ecclesiastical history and, also, poetry.

In all of his previous books, Taylor had invariably shown a rather strong antipathy to German politics and leaders. Hence, he could not logically be suspected of any pro-German sympathies or any desire to clear Hitler or any other German politician of political errors or public crimes which could be supported by reliable documentation. Finally, he has been closely associated with British left-wing activities, the Labor Party, disarmament, and other attitudes and policies which make it quite impossible for him to be imagined as having any sympathy with totalitarianism of any sort, least of all with that of national socialist Germany in the 1930s. Clement Attlee and the Laborites were, if anything, more vehement in their hatred of Hitler and so-called appeasement than the Tories who were in power in Britain in 1938–39.

Hence, it would be difficult to conceive of any historian who could give greater assurance that his criticisms of the dragon-slaying hypothesis are no more than those which historical accuracy and reliable documentation make necessary. They are a product of historical integrity and professional courage, probably more of the latter than has been displayed by any other historian of our generation. It is interesting to note that since his book on the causes of the Second World War has appeared, a number of critical reviewers have accused Taylor of being a publicity-seeking vendor of sensationalism who must not be taken seriously as a historian. But these same critics are usually the very ones who had previously applauded his profound scholarship when his books reflected a strong hostility to Germany and its policies.

After these preliminary observations, which are indispensable for judging the importance and validity of Professor Taylor's work, we can now get down to the outstanding conclusions which are expressed in the book.

The vital core of the volume is the contention that Hitler did not wish a war, either local, European, or world, from March 1933 right down into September 1939. His only fundamental aim in foreign policy was to revise the unfair and unjust Treaty of Versailles, and to do this by peaceful methods.

This is a most remarkable and unusual contention, however well defended in the book. Hitherto, even those who have sympathized heartily with the justice and need of revising the Versailles Treaty have, nevertheless, usually maintained that, even if Hitler's revisionist program was justified in its general objectives, he carried it out in a reprehensibly brusque, provocative, and challenging manner, gladly or casually risking war in each and every move he made to achieve the revision of the Versailles system. In other words, even if his goal was justifiable, his methods of seeking to obtain it were unpardonably violent, deceitful, and inciting.

Professor Taylor repudiates and refutes the interpretation as thoroughly as he does the charge that Hitler wished to provoke war at any time. He holds that Hitler was unusually cautious and unprovocative in every outstanding step he took to undermine

Versailles. He let others create situations favorable to achieving his ends and then exploited them in a nonbellicose manner.

One thing is certain, even if one takes a most hostile attitude towards Hitler and Professor Taylor's thesis. This is that the Allies had some thirteen years in which to revise the Treaty of Versailles in a voluntary and peaceful manner. But they did nothing about it, although one of the main ostensible functions of the League of Nations was stated to be carrying forward a peaceable revision of Versailles. Professor Sidney B. Fay had proved by 1920 that the war-guilt clause of the Treaty of Versailles, proclaiming that Germany and her allies were solely responsible for the First World War, had no valid historical foundation whatever.

Professor Fay and the rest of us revisionists of the 1920s hoped that since the facts we brought forth had completely undermined the war-guilt clause, this would lead to the revision of the treaty in political fact. But it did not, and the failure to do so accounts for the rise of Hitler and all the many results for good or evil which ensued.

After he came into power, Hitler waited patiently for some years for the Allies to make some practical move to revise the Versailles system before he occupied the Rhineland on March 7, 1936. Even on the heels of this action he publicly proposed on March 31, 1936, what Francis Neilson has called "the most comprehensive nonaggression pact ever to be drawn up." But the Allies made no cooperative response whatever; they totally ignored it. They accused him of bluffing but refused to call his bluff, if it was such.

Hitler had barely attained power when, on May 17, 1933, he proposed the most sweeping disarmament plan set forth by any country between the two world wars, but neither Britain nor France took any formal notice whatever of it. Even after he had introduced conscription in March 1935 in response to the expansion of military conscription in France, Hitler declared that "the German government is ready to take an active part in all efforts which may lead to a practical limitation of armaments." This proposal received no more response from Britain, France, or the United States than that of May 1933. Hence, if Hitler was to revise Versailles at all, it had become completely evident by March 1936 that it must be by unilateral action.

We should always keep in mind Taylor's fundamental assumption about Hitler, to the effect that he was not a fanatical and bellicose psychopath—a veritable madman intent upon war—but a shrewd and rational statesman, notably in his handling of foreign affairs.

It will hardly be necessary for any sane person to emphasize the fact that Professor Taylor does not seek to present Hitler as any combination of Little Lord Fauntleroy, George Washington at the cherry tree, Clara Barton, and Jane Addams. He could be as devious, shrewd, inconsistent, self-contradictory, cruel, and brutal as the leaders among his enemies, although he did balk at saturation bombing of civilians until he was compelled by Britain to do so in retaliation. The main point here is that, unlike Churchill, Roosevelt, and Stalin, he did not wish to have a war break out in 1939.

It is very important to indicate briefly the significance of the book by Professor Taylor for citizens of the United States. So far as revisionist scholarship is concerned, this is greatly strengthened and its basic contentions are confirmed. It should now be easier to treat the causes of the Second World War realistically and honestly without being accused of mental defect or moral depravity.

The awe and reverence with which English historians are customarily regarded by the American historical guild should make it the more difficult and embarrassing for the latter to laugh off Professor Taylor's confirmation of the basic tenets of American revisionist historical scholarship. The frenetic reviews of the book have already revealed the schizoid reaction of American antirevisionists—a sort of intellectual "twist" dance.

The Taylor book underlines the wisdom and soundness of American anti-interventionism which had been supported by revisionist historical writings in this country. The interventionists based their policy on the fantastic assumption, actually voiced by such able historians as Samuel Flagg Bemis, earlier a mild revisionist, top commentators like Walter Lippmann, and superb journalists of the type of Walter Millis, that the United States was in mortal danger of infiltration and attack by Nazi Germany in 1940.

The flipflopping and inconsistency of much of this interpretation is well illustrated by Millis who, in a book entitled *Viewed Without Alarm: Europe Today,* published as late as 1937, had attacked warmongers and alarmists, commended British "appeasement" of Hitler, and looked forward sympathetically to future

German unification of Central Europe: "If the Nazis can create a growing economic and social system in Central Europe, it will be —however unpleasant for the lesser nations it swallows—not a menace but a market and a stabilizing force for the rest of the world" (p. 53). It may be observed that this envisaged German expansion beyond anything Hitler had attained at the time war broke out in September 1939.

Professor Taylor's book emphasizes the grosteque fallacy of this alarmist contention relative to the national socialist program of world conquest. Hitler did not even wish to attack England or France, to say nothing of proceeding westward across the Atlantic. Nor was it necessary for the United States to enter the war to protect Britain or France. Hitler sought peace on very generous terms after the Polish war and again after the fall of France, and the British collapse at Dunkirk.

In the light of the facts brought forward by Professor Taylor, which are not at all new to American revisionist historians and had previously been well stated by Tansill, Beard, and others, President Roosevelt's allegation that Hitler planned to invade the United States by way of Dakar, Rio de Janeiro, and Panama—his notorious timetable for the Nazi occupation of Iowa—is shown to be as fantastic and untenable as his statement that he was "surprised" by the Japanese attack in December 1941.

Professor Taylor's book should serve as a warning that a third world war will not be prevented by an avalanche of stale and exaggerated Germanophobia, or by merely mouthing arrogant platitudes and benign homilies about the virtues and superiorities of democracy and the "free world," as was the habit of Cordell Hull. These semantic gestures must be supplemented and implemented by all the wisdom, precaution, foresight, and statecraft that can be drawn from the disastrous experience with two world wars and their ominous aftermaths. Failing this, we are not likely to have another opportunity.

We are not likely to succeed so long as we resolutely reject searching self-examination but continue to seek a scapegoat on whom we may lay the blame for all international tragedies. The effort to make a scapegoat out of the kaiser and Germany after the First World War produced the Versailles Treaty and, in time, the Second World War. The same process was continued on a more fantastic scale after the Second World War, and it has already led us to the brink of nuclear war several times. Professor Taylor has made clear the folly in seeking to make Hitler's foreign policy the cause of all the miseries and anguish of the world since 1939—or even 1933.

We can get no valid comfort from the illusion that nuclear warfare will be withheld in the third world war, as poison gas was in the second. As F. J. P. Veale pointed out so well in his *Advance to Barbarism,* the Nuremberg trials took care of that. These showed that the rule in the future will be that defeated leaders, military and civilian, will be executed. Hence, no leader in wartime will spare any available and effective horrors which may avert defeat. Field Marshall Bernard Law Montgomery got this point when he stated in Paris in June 1948: "The Nuremberg trials have made the waging of unsuccessful war a crime: the generals on the defeated side are tried and then hanged." He should have added chiefs of state, prime ministers, foreign ministers, and even secretaries of welfare.

While it is easy to demonstrate that the Second World War and American entry into it constituted one of the outstanding public calamities in human history, and perhaps the last—surely, the next to the last—of such magnitude, the question is always asked as to what *should* have been done. There is no space here to write a treatise on world history or to combine prophesy with hindsight. But a reasonable answer can be suggested.

Britain should not have started the Second World War. The British leaders knew that Hitler was no threat to them. Next to assuring German strength, he was mainly interested in bolstering the British empire. As Liddell Hart and others have shown, even after Dunkirk he offered to put the German *Wehrmacht* and *Luftwaffe* at the service of Britain if she would make peace.

Germany and Russia had made a pact in August 1939, and both were interested in turning east and south. If they remained friendly, they could have developed and civilized these great untamed areas and would have reduced their interests in the West. If they quarreled and fought, they would thereby have reduced the two great totalitarian systems to impotence through military attrition. Once the war started and Germany had invaded Russia, Britain and the United States should have remained aloof and allowed these totalitarian rivals to bleed themselves white and thereby end their menace to the Western world.

The wisdom of such procedure was recognized by public leaders in both major political parties, such as ex-President Herbert Hoover, Senator Robert A. Taft, and Senator Harry S. Truman. Had their advice been heeded, communism would not now dominate a vast portion of the planet or have over a billion adherents. Nor would we be faced with a war of nuclear extermination.

But the combined power of Roosevelt's lust for the glamor of a war presidency, the Communist line about "collective security," so successfully propounded by Litvinov at Geneva and adopted by American liberals as the ideological basis of their interventionism, and Churchill's gargantuan vanity and vast enjoyment of his prestige as wartime leader, was far too great to be overcome by either factual information or political logic. The dolorous results of the folly of American intervention and Roosevelt's concessions to Stalinite communism still dominate the material on world affairs in every daily newspaper and every political journal of our time.

The schizoid confusion and consternation of American antirevisionist historians when facing the contentions and conclusions of the Taylor book were well illustrated by their reviews in leading historical journals, of which the *American Historical Review* holds first place. Among these historians, one of the most distinguished and aggressive is Professor Raymond J. Sontag of the eminent University of California in Berkeley, California. Professor Sontag reviewed the Taylor book in the July 1962 issue of the *American Historical Review.* He had been a frank revisionist with respect to the First World War, and had written to me pleasantly, even flatteringly, concerning my *Genesis of the World War.* It was well known, however, that he had undergone a great change in attitude in approaching the background of 1939 but few could have been prepared for his review of the Taylor book. It was a superficial smear from beginning to end and made no attempt whatever to indicate the nature, significance, and contributions of the book as the first revisionist treatment of the causes of the Second World War to appear in any language. There was no real excuse for such an exhibition because Sontag had been one of the principal supervisors and editors of the documents on 1939 seized from the Germans at the end of the war.

Sontag attacked Taylor vigorously for condensing slightly some of the cited documentary material although this did not seem to have made any real difference in Taylor's interpretation of the essentials of his case. He then proceeded to offer some largely irrelevant and casuistic criticism of details, such as Taylor's not regarding Hitler's *Mein Kampf* and other early statements as valid evidence of his plans in 1938–1939. All this could be overlooked, even though much better use could have been made of the space thus taken up by giving readers of the review some slight idea of the character, originality, merits, and contributions of the book. What cannot be regarded so complacently is that Sontag then completely misrepresented the basic thesis of Taylor's book by contending that Taylor treats British policy after the German demand for the return of Danzig on March 21, 1939, as "foolish, blindly foolish" and responsible for dragging Europe into the tragedy of war.

The fact is that Taylor declares several times that no country wanted war in 1939 and that it was the product of blunders by all. The main weakness and defect of the Taylor book is actually his palpable failure adequately to reveal the responsibility of Britain for the onset of the war. In a brochure on Taylor's book, entitled "Blasting the Historical Blackout," I devoted some twenty-one pages to a careful analysis of the content and contentions of the volume. I found it necessary to devote no less than eight of these pages to a summary of the evidence indicating that Taylor actually absolved Britain of any direct or major responsibility for the onset of war during the critical period from the end of March to early September, 1939. Apparently, Sontag regards it as highly reprehensible to juggle the text of a few documents, even if this does not materially affect the author's narrative or generalizations, but quite permissible, even commendable, to juggle a whole book and totally misrepresent its main argument and conclusions.

The confusion and contradictions involved in the efforts of anti-interventionist historians in facing up to a realistic treatment of the facts about responsibility for the Second World War were further revealed in an article that Professor Sontag wrote in the *Review of Politics,* October 1963, on this subject. The main contention of this article was that determining the responsibility for the coming of war in 1939 is so complicated and difficult that the problem is not likely to be settled in a definitive manner for many years to come. This is a defensible assertion. Yet, he also concludes that the responsibility of Hitler and the Germans for 1939 is

so obvious that its demonstration does not require serious historical investigation.

Revisionism and Peace

A chief reason why any friend of peace should be warmly interested in the revisionist verdict on the responsibility for the Second
World War and American entry into the conflict is that it destroys
the fatal illusion that the only danger of war after the Treaty of
Versailles lay in the aggressive nature of the German people and
their leaders, and that destroying them would surely usher in a
glorious era of brotherly love, in which swords would literally be
beaten into plowshares.

As Russell Grenfell did well to point out in his vigorous and
courageous book, *Unconditional Hatred,* it is doubtful if ever
before in history "have so many aggressions been crowded into so
short a time as have taken place in the years since the defeat of
Germany and Japan." Mankind has never been able to hate
humanity into peace but, under the present conditions of military
technology, nations can, and possibly will, hate each other into
extinction.

Mention of Captain Grenfell suggests that far the most important point relative to the Second World War and the "peace"
which followed has been very generally overlooked, even by most
revisionists including myself. Yet, it is absolutely indispensable to
drawing the main lesson for any constructive pacifism in the future, if there is to be any future. Grenfell criticized Churchill for
trying to act like a "Whitehall Napoleon" rather than a sagacious
"Downing Street statesman." This was a shrewd observation, but
General Albert C. Wedemeyer has correctly contended that even
this characterization of Churchill's conduct of the war is actually
too kindly a judgment, for "he waged war more like an Indian
chieftain from the Arizona territory intent upon obtaining the
largest possible number of enemy scalps." He goes on to say with
equal accuracy: "Our own leaders were just as vehement in proclaiming that the slaughter of the enemy was a primary aim of the
war."

This matter is of fundamental importance for pacifism and the
cause of peace because it bears so very directly upon the wide-

spread complaint that, while the Allies "won the *war,* they lost the *peace.*" This is usually coupled with the assertion that the peace was lost chiefly because of the "unconditional surrender" policy and related actions and attitudes which ignored the inevitable results of concentration on sheer butchery and hollow military triumph, and forgot the need of planning for a better and more peaceful world after the victory was won, as had been stated in the Atlantic Charter of August 1941. Nobody has more frequently repeated this actually superficial view of the situation than myself.

The plain and blunt fact is that, in the Second World War, the Allies had no *peace* to lose from the very moment that the conflict started. The British entered the war to "smash Germany" and to destroy Hitler and the Nazis. Roosevelt and the Americans adopted the identical program at once, merely adding the smashing of Japan. Stalin was compelled to take it over because he had been attacked by Germany, whatever the merits of the struggle between the two countries. All three countries were thus committed to a global "scalping party." There were no actual *peace* aims or program. All the aims were *war* aims. The purpose of the war was to kill Germans, Japanese, and Italians. Stalin added to this the acquisition of territory and peoples that would act as a protective buffer against any powerful Germany of the future and also, he hoped, assure Russian hegemony in the Old World.

To be successful the "scalping party" literally required "unconditional surrender," even if it had never been specifically announced by Roosevelt at Casablanca. Indeed, the British had adopted this policy from the very outbreak of the war on September 3, 1939. The Atlantic Charter was dead before the ink was dry on the proceedings at Newfoundland. It had no role in a scalping party. In fact, Churchill knew it was doomed before he met Roosevelt there, for it ran counter to the British reasons for starting the war and Stalin had already demanded the spoils of victory from Britain before he had been willing to discuss any basic strategy for winning the victory. The Allies won just exactly what they fought for—and *all* they fought for: an astronomical number of enemy scalps and incredible physical destruction of enemy property and homes, together with great territorial and population acquisitions for Russia. They lost nothing whatever for which they had actually planned and fought. It is a travesty to condemn them for losing the *peace*—something they never really had in mind. They can, of course, be condemned for having little or nothing except butchery and destruction (save in the case of Stalin) on their minds.

Pacifists who overlook these fundamental facts ignore the most important lesson to be drawn from the Second World War and one that has to be faced even more urgently today. These facts demonstrate for all time the complete political and moral bankruptcy of the Second World War, and it would have been just as savage and futile if the concentration had been on killing Britishers, Frenchmen, Russians, or Americans. In the cold war of today, we face even greater public idiocy and potential calamity. In the Second World War, it was only a matter of killing Germans, Japanese, and Italians; today, we are confronted with the prospect of killing everybody on the planet with no basic plans or motives other than a "massive surprise attack," to be followed by the mopping up of survivors through a "massive retaliation."

The origins and motives of the cold war were as sordid and ethically bankrupt as those of the Second World War: Stalin's determination to hold his illicit gains, the British effort to regain their balance-of-power position which they had lost in the war that was designed by Halifax and the British war group to preserve it, and the effort of Truman and Clark Clifford to pull the Democratic political prospects out of the subbasement of opinion ratings in late February 1947. There was evidently the same collaboration between Truman and the British in 1946–47 as there had been between Roosevelt and the British between 1938 and 1941. The Republican bipartisan support of the cold war, engineered by Arthur Vandenberg and his cohorts, was no less selfish and sordid.

The world was soon consigned to the operational framework of the Orwellian pattern of linking up bogus economic prosperity and political tenure with cold and phony warfare, from which the only relief may well be devastating nuclear warfare, set off by design or accident, and in either case surely killing off more in the first hours than were killed in the whole Second World War. In the meantime we linger along, continuing the series of lesser tactical or revolutionary "hot wars" in Korea, South Vietnam, the Congo, and elsewhere, which are so needed to stoke the fires of our military state capitalistic economy. Indeed, in *Time* of September 25, 1965, it was suggested in a lengthy and factual editorial that we might as well get adjusted to this situation of worldwide non-nuclear war as permanent until the final nuclear overkill comes along. In its issue of December 6, 1965, *U.S. News & World Report* amply documented this dolorous conclusion of *Time* in a comprehensive article entitled "The World in a Mess" and indicated that there are a dozen or more places where the United States could as logically be intervening as in South Vietnam and that such opportunities will not be lacking so long as this trend and policy dominates our global attitude.

The New Strategy in Maintaining the Historical Blackout on the Second World War: The Blurout and the Smotherout

The preceding review of the methods employed in producing a blackout relative to the causes of the Second World War and the American entry into the fray in December 1941, could make it appear that the results should have satisfied the proponents of the program to keep the facts from the conventional academic world and the American public. But this did not suffice. The facts might be kept from general knowledge but it became increasingly apparent that the factual material piled up by the revisionist scholars might not remain permanently suppressed. Some method must be found to minimize or destroy the relevance of these facts themselves.

The first device or technique which was employed to produce this result was what has-been called by revisionist scholars the "historical blurout." This method was most notably exemplified by the book of Dr. Roberta Wohlstetter, *Pearl Harbor: Warning and Decision,* published in 1962. Little attempt was made in this book to deny or refute the basic facts established by revisionist writers from Morgenstern until the present time. Instead, a great number of distracting, secondary, or irrelevant items were brought in with respect to the critical matters in the hope that these would obscure or blur out the recognition or import of the really vital facts or conclusions established by revisionist scholars. This sufficed to satisfy many of the traditional blackout contingent. Samuel Eliot Morison declared Dr. Wohlstetter's book to be "the best book by far on the question of why we were surprised at Pearl Harbor," and it was reviewed in a similar lyrical vein in most of the historical journals and the book review sections of leading newspapers.

Nevertheless, the blurout technique did not satisfy the more farsighted and determined members of the blackout cult. Too many revisionist contentions were admitted and shrewd revisionists could penetrate the blurring stratagem. Moreover, it was not so well adapted to handling the responsibility for the outbreak of war in Europe in 1939 which is, after all, the most crucial aspect of revisionism in relation to the Second World War. Some method had to be devised to make it appear that even though revisionists might demonstrate that Hitler was not solely responsible for the Second World War, that the responsibility of Britain was greater, and that Roosevelt deliberately forced Japan into a situation that made Japanese military resistance to economic strangulation inevitable, these major contentions of revisionism are of subordinate significance, if not actually irrelevant. To produce this result, the blurout technique was expanded or really supplanted by what can best be described as the "historical smotherout." This is rapidly becoming the technique of those directing the strategy of combating revisionism and it promises to be far more effective than the historical blackout in suppressing revisionist efforts to establish and disseminate the truth relative to responsibility for the Second World War and American entry into the conflict.

The feasibility and effectiveness of this new strategy appears to have been suggested by the Eichmann trial of 1961. This demonstrated the apparently intense and insatiable appetite of American readers for anything which emphasized national socialist savagery, an opportunity which our communications agencies exploited to the uttermost. This morbid interest was prolonged and stimulated by the Frankfurt-Auschwitz trial, which was so planned as to drag on for an entire year, after which the West Germans were pressured into lifting their statute of limitations on war crimes, thus making it possible to continue such trials indefinitely.

The smotherout strategy, which has supplanted the previous procedure that dominated the efforts to counteract revisionism for a decade and a half after the end of hostilities, has now shifted attention from primary concern with responsibility for the beginning of the war and for American entry, to establishing the basic assumption that what really matters is what took place *after* hostilities were started. The fundamental aim has now become to emphasize the allegation that Hitler and the national socialist leaders were such vile, debased, brutal, and bloodthirsty gangsters that Great Britain had an overwhelming moral obligation to plan a war to exterminate them, and that the United States was compelled to enter this conflict to aid and abet this British crusade because of a moral imperative that could not be evaded to engage in a campaign of political, social, and cultural sanitation.

To implement and reinforce this new smotherout strategy, American journalism, radio, motion pictures, and television have been flooded with profuse and persistent alleged examples and "proofs" of national socialist turpitude and Hitler's personal diabolism, far exceeding anything known in wartime and ever increasing in frequency, volume, and venom. Lest the public become "fed up" and bored by the repetition, the material handed out has to be made more unceasing, exaggerated, and inflammatory. Scholarly revisionist materials are smothered beneath a flood of sensational horror literature. Even the literate public only gets into contact with scattered and minor bits of substantial revisionist material at considerable intervals. But not a day goes by without one or more sensational articles appearing in the daily papers about the national socialist savagery which required Britain to start the war and the United States to enter it, the weekly and monthly journals never miss their quota of this passionate prose, the radio has it on the air daily, expensive moving pictures are devoted to the theme, not a week passes by without several inciting television programs revolving about this intensified propaganda, and lurid books pour forth at frequent intervals.

It was difficult enough for revisionist writers to make headway against the older historical blackout in the form of the silent treatment, grossly distorted reviews, incessant smearing and the like, but revisionism is now becoming smothered and obliterated by this new technique of diversionary sensationalism. It cannot be resisted or countered by accurate diplomatic history, which is now implied to be no more than "piddling" irrelevance, savoring of a lack of moral sensitivity. To expect the public to listen to sober revisionist scholarship in the face of the current avalanche of violent vituperation against prewar and wartime Germany is like imagining a housewife whose home is on fire and the flames threatening her small children, being eager or even willing to open her door to a Fuller Brush salesman and listen intently to his sales talk. If an antirevisionist or nonrevisionist scholar is approached with the assertion that it is no longer possible to maintain the sole guilt of Germany in 1939 or the notion that Roosevelt entered the war reluctantly in December 1941 and was surprised and shocked by the Japanese attack, the response is increasingly becoming: ''So what? Look at what those subhuman Nazis did after the war got started, no matter who started it!''

This diversion of the debate over the revisionist approach to the Second World War from the area of historical documentation and discussion to frenetic and irresponsible emotional journalism, whether in print, on the air, or in films, has now become the Hindenburg Line of the existing resistance to revisionism. It may well be the last redoubt of the defenders of historical fiction and mendacity, but it also appears all but inevitable that it may be relatively impregnable and permanent, not because of its validity but on account of the fact that any attempt to launch an attack based on fact and logic will be fiercely, ruthlessly, and speedily smothered and discounted. Those most eager to perpetuate the historical blackout operating under this new pattern and strategy already have a tight control, directly or indirectly, over all the means of communication. This control may not be shaken off short of some now completely unforeseen and revolutionary political alignment of the world, or of such a universal and drastic development of totalitarianism and intolerance as to elevate Hitler, even among the opponents of this trend, into much the same role and status that Thomas Jefferson has long enjoyed among American liberals, a prospect by no means impossible.

That the strategists of the new model blackout or smotherout are confident of indefinite control of communication agencies is apparent from the fact that the current massive and virulent Germanophobia is far easier to refute than the documentary opposition to revisionism. Even if one were to accept the most extreme and exaggerated indictment of Hitler and the national socialists for their activities after 1939 made by anybody fit to remain outside a mental hospital, it is almost alarmingly easy to demonstrate that the atrocities of the Allies in the same period were more numerous as to victims and were carried out for the most part by methods more brutal and painful than alleged extermination in gas ovens.

To look for a moment at the Communist atrocities, between

three and four million German expellees lost their lives through overt butchery, lethal brutality, and starvation during the process. The Yugoslav publicist, Mihajlo Mihajlov, examining Russian sources in 1964, revealed that at least twelve millions passed through Stalin's concentration camps, with untold mortality and suffering, to say nothing of the great number of Russian refugees deported from Germany to Russia for slaughter or enslavement at the close of hostilities.

The infamous Lindemann plan for saturation bombing of German civilians which was quickly adopted by Churchill and the British, matches for moral depravity and inhuman cruelty anything alleged against Hitler and the German concentration camps. If the current Germanophobia is based on the assertion that Hitler and his entourage ordered the extermination of six million Jews, there is no doubt that the Morgenthau plan for postwar Germany envisaged the starvation of twenty to thirty million Germans in transforming Germany into a pastoral country. This plan was enthusiastically adopted by Roosevelt, and Churchill was bribed into supporting it. No action seriously alleged against Hitler and his subordinates surpasses for casual and needless brutality the incendiary bombings of Tokyo and Hamburg or the destruction of Dresden.

All other indefensible breaches of a humane code by either Hitler or the Allies were outdistanced by the atom bombings of Hiroshima and Nagasaki more than six months after the Japanese had virtually sued for peace on the same terms that were accepted on V-J Day after the atom bombings, which the noted British military authority General J. F. C. Fuller denounced as gratuitous savagery unmatched since the days of Genghis Khan and Tamerlane. We now know that those responsible for ordering the atom bombings, especially Secretary of War Stimson, were fully aware that the Japanese were desperately eager to surrender and that the bombings were not necessary to bring immediate peace. The documents now available prove that the bombings were ordered and were approved by Stimson as technological exhibitionism and were carried out primarily to impress and intimidate the Russians.

The neo-blackout or smotherout strategists would not dare to invite a disastrous showdown and the exposure of their methods and contentions if they did not feel certain that they can indefinitely smother the presentation of the material which would so easily refute their mendacity. Any revisionist protests or corrections in relation to the recent blatant and irresponsible Germanophobia are met by charges of anti-Semitism or an intention to "rehabilitate" Hitler, despite the fact that there has not been one anti-Semite or Hitler sympathizer among all the American revisionist historians. Indeed, most of them have been at least moderate Judophiles and severe critics of Hitler and national socialism.

Further evidence that the custodians of the new pattern of smotherout strategy feel confident of retaining indefinite control of publishing and communication agencies, and that the latter will continue their eagerness to serve their present masters, is to be discerned in the apparently utter indifference to a possible drastic backlash, if and when the blackout and smotherout are ultimately demolished and the truth is made available, which would rapidly be the case if revisionists ever gained even decent access to our publishing and communication facilities. Being for the most part literate persons, the hierarchy of the new smotherout dispensation must surely recall the revulsion which followed the revelation by Abrams, Lasswell, Mock and Larson, Peterson, Ponsonby, and Read of the hoax perpetrated by the Bryce report on alleged German atrocities during the First World War. But the Bryce report and wartime propaganda of that era were only a trifling deviation from veracity as compared with much of the current Germanophobia.

Perhaps the leaders of the new smotherout strategy also reckon on the very possible loss of any capacity for moral revulsion or self-respect on the part of the American public. The fact that books like *The Quiet Canadian* and *Black Boomerang* could pass almost unnoticed may provide impressive evidence supporting this view. It required the books of outsiders like Arthur Ponsonby, J. M. Read, and others to expose the falsity of the Bryce report and comparable propaganda literature. Today, the masters of propaganda and mendacity in the Second World War proudly confess their malign achievements and boast of them. Whatever slight attention has been paid to their arrogance and audacity has mainly partaken of praise rather than public shame, indignation, and denunciation.

Professor Michael Connors will deal more thoroughly with the rise and implications of the current Germanophobia for the revisionist movement; hence, little more need be said about it here.

The relevant fact is that opposition to revisionism in relation to the Second World War has been transformed in recent years from historical study and discussion into a loaded public propaganda enterprise. It has passed from the investigation and interpretation of documents and other traditional historical evidence into a frenzied concentration of publicity on extermination archeology, comparative biology, clinical pathology, and genocidal ethics, with no immediate prospect of exposure and disgrace for the smootherout fraud, because only one side has access to the publicity.

It is inevitable that a comparable change must be made in the pattern of revisionist procedure relative to the Second World War. It is no longer remotely possible to make effective headway in public, or even scholarly, debate. If the public could not be made aware of revisionist materials and induced to read them in the 1950s, there is surely little or no prospect of making headway in honest factual debate today in the face of the literal tornado of hostile and sensational bilge presented daily by our communication agencies.

Aside from the need of a few more comprehensive books to supplement that of Professor Taylor on the causes and responsibility for the Second World War, and perhaps a comprehensive book on Pearl Harbor to bring together the new evidence as to the responsibility of Roosevelt, Stimson, and Hull for the Japanese attack, thus supplementing Morgenstern's tour de force by the latest knowledge which confirms his main conclusions, the historical and factual battle of revisionism has been won. But the extensive revisionist literature on which this has been based and that which will be presented later on must be regarded for the time being as existing mainly for the record, prior to the time when historical facts can reach the public, unimpeded by censorship, mendacity, favoritism, and fraud. If this time never comes, the failure will be accompanied by far worse calamities to civilization and the human race than ignorance of the responsibility for the Second World War and American entry into it, even though these latter two events may constitute the main original basis for the abysmal calamities which can await us, including nuclear extermination. They have surely been chiefly responsible for most of the global disasters and demoralization which have arisen since 1939.

Future historical revisionist writing in the current intellectual temper and publicity scene must therefore be regarded as chiefly for the record, and we already have a monumental and impressive achievement for this new revisionist program: Professor James J. Martin's *American Liberalism and World Politics, 1931–1941,* which portrays the most stupendous betrayal of humane ideology and public morality in contemporary times. Others will follow.*

---

*My prediction that antirevisionism will in the future combine the smear technique of the earlier historical blackout with the Germanophobia of the new smotherout is strikingly confirmed by the review of Professor Martin's book by Professor Robert H. Ferrell of the University of Indiana in the *American Historical Review,* January 1966, pp. 728–730.

Ferrell smears the Martin book by describing it as a "scholarly disaster," offering no evidence for this except for indicating that he found the material unpleasant reading. He then amply provides the Germanophobia of the smotherout by describing the national socialist regime as the "most amoral government since the statistically clouded times of Genghis Khan."

The review further illustrates Professor Martin's contention that the "respectable" and traditional American historians of today are making the test of desirable prose not whether it is true but whether it makes pleasant reading to these historians and their brain-washed public.

Revisionism and
the Historical Blackout

The revisionist search for truth relative to the causes of the second World War is "serious, unfortunate, deplorable."
—SAMUEL FLAGG BEMIS, *Journal of Modern History,* March 1947

One thing ought to be evident to all of us: by our victory over Germany and Japan, no matter what our folly in losing the peace, we have at least survived to confront the second even greater menace of another totalitarian power.
—SAMUEL FLAGG BEMIS, *New York Times,* October 15, 1950

The folklore of war, of course, begins long before the fighting is done; and, by the time the last smoke has drifted away, this folklore has congealed into a "truth" of a neolithic hardness.
—STEWART H. HOLBROOK, *Lost Men of American History,* p. 42

How War Has Transformed
the American Dream into a Nightmare

The First World War and American intervention therein marked an ominous turning point in the history of the United States and of the world. Those who can remember "the good old days" before 1914 inevitably look back to those times with a very definite and justifiable feeling of nostalgia. There was no income tax before 1913, and that levied in the early days after the amendment was adopted was little more than nominal. All kinds of taxes were relatively low. We had only a token national debt of around a billion dollars, which could have been paid off in a year without causing even a ripple in national finance. The total federal budget in 1913 was $724,512,000, just about one percent of the present astronomical budget.

Ours was a libertarian country in which there was little or no witch-hunting and few of the symptoms and operations of the police state which have been developing here so drastically during the last decade. Not until our intervention in the First World War had there been sufficient invasions of individual liberties to call forth the formation of special groups and organizations to protect our civil rights. The Supreme Court could still be relied on to uphold the Constitution and safeguard the civil liberties of individual citizens.

Libertarianism was also dominant in Western Europe. The Liberal party governed England from 1905 to 1914. France had risen above the reactionary *coup* of the Dreyfus affair, had separated church and state, and had seemingly established the Third Republic with reasonable permanence on a democratic and liberal basis. Even Hohenzollern Germany enjoyed the usual civil liberties, had strong constitutional restraints on executive tyranny, and had established a workable system of parliamentary government. Experts on the history of Austria-Hungary have recently been proclaiming that life in the Dual Monarchy after the turn of the century marked the happiest period in the experience of the peoples encompassed therein. Constitutional government, democracy, and civil liberties prevailed in Italy. Despite the suppression of the Liberal Revolution of 1905, liberal sentiment was making headway in czarist Russia, and there was decent prospect that a constitutional monarchy might be established. Civilized states expressed abhorrence of dictatorial and brutal policies. Edward VII of England blacklisted Serbia after the court murders of 1903.

Enlightened citizens of the Western world were then filled with buoyant hope for a bright future for humanity. It was believed that the theory of progress had been thoroughly vindicated by historical events. Edward Bellamy's *Looking Backward,* published in 1888, was the prophetic bible of that era.[1] People were confident that the amazing developments in technology would soon produce abundance, security, and leisure for the multitude.

In this optimism in regard to the future no item was more evident and potent than the assumption that war was an outmoded nightmare. Not only did idealism and humanity repudiate war, but Norman Angell and others were assuring us that war could not be justified, even on the basis of the most sordid material interest. Those who adopted a robust international outlook were devoted friends of peace, and virtually all international movements had as their sole aim the devising and implementing of ways

[1] New edition, Boston: Houghton Mifflin Company, 1941.

and means to assure permanent peace. Friends of peace were no-where isolationist in any literal sense, but they did stoutly uphold the principle of neutrality and sharply criticized provocative med-dling in every political dogfight in the most remote reaches of the planet.

In our own country, the traditional American foreign policy of benign neutrality and the wise exhortations of George Washing-ton, Thomas Jefferson, John Quincy Adams and Henry Clay to avoid entangling alliances and to shun foreign quarrels were still accorded respect in the highest councils of state.

Unfortunately, there are relatively few persons today who can recall those happy times. In his devastatingly prophetic book, *Nineteen Eighty-Four,*[2] George Orwell points out that one reason why it is possible for those in authority to maintain the barbarities of the police state is that nobody is able to recall the many bless-ings of the period which preceded that type of society. In a general way this is also true of the peoples of the Western world today. The great majority of them have known only a world ravaged by war, depressions, international intrigues and meddling, vast debts and crushing taxation, the encroachments of the police state, and the control of public opinion and government by ruthless and ir-responsible propaganda. A major reason why there is no revolt against such a state of society as that in which we are living today is that many have come to accept it as a normal matter of course, having known nothing else during their lifetimes.

A significant and illuminating report on this situation came to me recently in a letter from one of the most distinguished social scientists in the country and a resolute revisionist. He wrote: "I am devoting my seminar this quarter to the subject of American foreign policy since 1933. The effect upon a Roosevelt-bred gener-ation is startling, indeed. Even able and mature students react to the elementary facts like children who have just been told that there is (or was) no Santa Claus." This is also an interesting reflection on the teaching of history today. The members of the seminar were graduate students, nearly all of whom had taken courses in recent American and European history which covered in some detail the diplomacy of Europe and the United States dur-ing the last twenty years.

[2]New York: Harcourt, Brace & Company, 1949. See especially pp. 86–93.

A friend who read the preceding material suggested that laboring men would be likely to give me a "horselaugh." That some would is no doubt true, but the essential issue would be the validity of the grounds for so doing. Being a student of the history of labor problems, I am aware of many gains for labor since 1914. I can well remember when the working day was ten hours long and the pay was $1.50. But I can also remember when good steak cost fifteen cents a pound and the best whisky eighty-five cents a quart. Moreover, the father, even if he earned only $1.50 a day, had every assurance that he could raise his family with his sons free from the shadow of the draft and butchery in behalf of politicians. The threat of war did not hang over him. There are some forms of tyranny worse than that of an arbitrary boss in a non-union shop. Finally, when one considers the increased cost of living and the burden of taxation, it is doubtful if a man who earns $8.00 a day now is any better off materially than his father or grandfather who earned $1.50 in 1900.

For the sad state of the world today, the entry of the United States into two world wars has played a larger role than any other single factor. Some might attribute the admittedly unhappy conditions of our time to other items and influences than world wars and our intervention in them. No such explanation can be sustained. Indeed, but for our entry into the two world wars, we should be living in a far better manner than we did before 1914. The advances in technology since that time have brought the automobile into universal use, have given us good roads, and have produced the airplane, radio, moving pictures, television, electric lighting and refrigeration, and numerous other revolutionary contributions to human service, happiness, and comforts. If all this had been combined with the freedom, absence of high taxation, minimum indebtedness, low armament expenditures, and pacific outlook of pre-1914 times, the people of the United States might, right now, be living in utopian security and abundance.

A radio commentator recently pointed out that one great advantage we have today over 1900 is that death from disease has been reduced and life expectancy considerably increased. But this suggests the query as to whether this is any real gain, in the light of present world conditions: Is it an advantage to live longer in a world of "thought-policing," economic austerity, crushing taxation, inflation, and perpetual warmongering and wars?

The rise and influence of Communism, military state capitalism, the police state, and the impending doom of civilization, have been the penalty exacted for our meddling abroad in situations which did not materially affect either our security or our prestige. Our national security was not even remotely threatened in the case of either world war. There was no clear moral issue impelling us to intervene in either world conflict. The level of civilization was lowered rather than elevated by our intervention.

While the First World War headed the United States and the world toward international disaster, the Second World War was an even more calamitous turning point in the history of mankind. It may, indeed, have brought us—and the whole world—into the terminal episode of human experience. It certainly marked the transition from social optimism and technological rationalism into the "Nineteen Eighty-Four" pattern of life, in which aggressive international policies and war scares have become the guiding factor, not only in world affairs but also in the domestic, political, and economic strategy of every leading country of the world. The police state has emerged as the dominant political pattern of our times, and military state capitalism is engulfing both democracy and liberty in countries which have not succumbed to Communism.

The manner and extent to which American culture has been impaired and our well-being undermined by our entry into two world wars has been brilliantly and succinctly stated by Professor Mario A. Pei of Columbia University in an article on "The America We Lost" in the *Saturday Evening Post*, May 3, 1952, and has been developed more at length by Garet Garrett in his trenchant book, *The People's Pottage*.

Perhaps, by the midcentury, all this is now water under the bridge and little can be done about it. But we can surely learn how we got into this unhappy condition of life and society—at least until the police-state system continues its current rapid development sufficiently to obliterate all that remains of integrity and accuracy in historical writing and political reporting.

Revisionism after Two World Wars

The readjustment of historical writing to historical facts relative to the background and causes of the First World War—what is popularly known in the historical craft as "revisionism"—was the most important development in historiography during the decade of the 1920s. While those historians at all receptive to the facts admitted that revisionism readily won out in the conflict with the previously accepted wartime lore, many of the traditionalists in the profession remained true to the mythology of the war decade. Not so long ago one of the most eminent and revered of our professional historians, and a man who took a leading part in historical propaganda during the First World War, wrote that American historians had no reason to feel ashamed of their writings and operations in that period. That they had plenty to be ashamed of was revealed by C. Hartley Grattan in his article "The Historians Cut Loose" in the *American Mercury*,[3] reprinted in the form originally submitted to Mr. Mencken in my *In Quest of Truth and Justice*,[4] and by Chapter XI of my *History of Historical Writing*.[5] In any event, the revisionist controversy was the outstanding intellectual adventure in the historical field in the twentieth century down to Pearl Harbor.

Revisionism, when applied to the First World War, showed that the actual causes and merits of that conflict were very close to the reverse of the picture presented in the political propaganda and historical writings of the war decade. Revisionism would also produce similar results with respect to the Second World War if it were allowed to develop unimpeded. But a determined effort is being made to stifle or silence revelations which would establish the truth with regard to the causes and issues of the late world conflict.

While the wartime mythology endured for years after 1918, nevertheless leading editors and publishers soon began to crave contributions which set forth the facts with respect to the responsibility for the outbreak of war in 1914, our entry into the war, and the basic issues involved in this great conflict. Sidney B. Fay began to publish his revolutionary articles on the background of the First World War in the *American Historical Review* in July 1920. My own efforts along the same line began in the *New Republic*, the *Nation*, the *New York Times Current History Magazine*, and the

[3] August 1927.
[4] Chicago: National Historical Society, 1928, pp. 142 ff.
[5] Norman, Okla.: University of Oklahoma Press, 1937.

Christian Century in 1924 and 1925. Without exception, the requests for my contributions came from the editors of these periodicals, and these requests were ardent and urgent. I had no difficulty whatever in securing the publication of my *Genesis of the World War* in 1926, and the publisher thereof subsequently brought forth a veritable library of illuminating revisionist literature. By 1928, when Fay's *Origins of the World War*[6] was published, almost everyone except the die-hards and bitter-enders in the historical profession had come to accept revisionism, and even the general public had begun to think straight in the premises.

Quite a different situation faces the rise of any substantial revisionism after the Second World War. The question of war responsibility in relation to 1939 and 1941 is taken for granted as completely and forever settled. It is widely held that there can be no controversy this time. Since it is admitted by all reasonable persons that Hitler was a dangerous neurotic, who, with supreme folly, launched a war when he had everything to gain by peace, it is assumed that this takes care of the European aspects of the war-guilt controversy. With respect to the Far East, this is supposed to be settled with equal finality by asking the question: "Japan attacked us, didn't she?"

About as frequent as either of these ways of settling war responsibility for 1939 or 1941 is the vague but highly dogmatic statement that "we had to fight." This judgment is usually rendered as a sort of ineffable categorical imperative which requires no further explanation. But some who are pressed for an explanation will allege that we had to fight to save the world from domination by Hitler, forgetting General George C. Marshall's report that Hitler, far from having any plan for world domination, did not even have any well-worked-out plan for collaborating with his Axis allies in limited wars, to say nothing of the gigantic task of conquering Russia. Surely, after June 22, 1941, nearly six months before Pearl Harbor, there was no further need to fear any world conquest by Hitler.

Actually, if historians have any professional self-respect and feel impelled to take cognizance of facts, there is far greater need for a robust and aggressive campaign of revisionism after the Sec-

[6]New York: The Macmillan Company, 1928.

ond World War than there was in the years following 1918. The current semantic folklore about the responsibility for the Second World War which is accepted, not only by the public but also by most historians, is far wider of the truth than even the most fantastic historical mythology which was produced after 1914. And the practical need for revisionism is even greater now than it was in the decade of the 1920s.

The mythology which followed the outbreak of war in 1914 helped to produce the Treaty of Versailles and the Second World War. If world policy today cannot be divorced from the mythology of the 1940s, a third world war is inevitable, and its impact will be many times more horrible and devastating than that of the second. The lessons learned from the Nuremberg and Tokyo trials have made it certain that the third world war will be waged with unprecedented savagery.

Vigorous as was the resistance of many, including powerful vested historical interests, to the revisionism of the 1920s, it was as nothing compared to that which has been organized to frustrate and smother the truth relative to the Second World War. Revisionists in the 1920s only risked a brisk controversy; those of today place in jeopardy both their professional reputation and their very livelihood at the hands of the "Smearbund." History has been the chief intellectual casualty of the Second World War and the cold war which followed.

In many essential features, the United States has moved along into the "Nineteen Eighty-Four" pattern of intellectual life. But there is one important and depressing difference. In *Nineteen Eighty-Four* Mr. Orwell shows that historians in that regime have to be hired by the government and forced to falsify facts. In this country today, and it is also true of most other nations, many professional historians gladly falsify history quite voluntarily, and with no direct cost to the government. The ultimate and indirect cost may, of course, be a potent contribution to incalculable calamity.

It may be said, with great restraint, that never since the Middle Ages have there been so many powerful forces organized and alerted against the assertion and acceptance of historical truth as are active today to prevent the facts about the responsibility for the Second World War and its results from being made generally accessible to the American public. Even the great Rockefeller

Foundation frankly admits[7] the subsidizing of historians to antici-
pate and frustrate the development of any neo-revisionism in our
time. And the only difference between this foundation and several
others is that it has been more candid and forthright about its
policies. The Sloan Foundation later supplemented this Rockefeller grant. Charles Austin Beard summarized the implications of
such efforts with characteristic vigor:

> The Rockefeller Foundation and the Council on Foreign Relations
> ... intend to prevent, if they can, a repetition of what they call in
> the vernacular "the debunking journalistic campaign following
> World War I." Translated into precise English, this means that the
> Foundation and the Council do not want journalists or any other
> persons to examine too closely and criticize too freely the official
> propaganda and official statements relative to "our basic aims and
> activities" during World War II. In short, they hope that, among
> other things, the policies and measures of Franklin D. Roosevelt
> will escape in the coming years the critical analysis, evaluation and
> exposition that befell the policies and measures of Woodrow
> Wilson and the Entente Allies after World War I.[8]

As is the case with nearly all book publishers and periodicals,
the resources of the great majority of the foundations are available only to scholars and writers who seek to perpetuate wartime
legends and oppose revisionism. A good illustration is afforded
by my experience with the Alfred P. Sloan Foundation, which
helped to subsidize the book by Professors Langer and Gleason. I
mentioned this fact in the first edition of my brochure on *The
Court Historians versus Revisionism*. Thereupon I received a
courteous letter from Mr. Alfred J. Zurcher, director of the Sloan
Foundation, assuring me that the Sloan Foundation wished to be
absolutely impartial and to support historical scholarship on both
sides of the issue. He wrote in part: "About the last thing we wish
to do is to check and frustrate any sort of historical scholarship
since we believe that the more points of view brought to bear by
disciplined scholars upon the war or any other historical event is
in the public interest and should be encouraged."

In the light of this statement, I decided to take Mr. Zurcher at
his word. I had projected and encouraged a study of the foreign
policy of President Hoover, which appeared to me a very important and much needed enterprise, since it was during his adminis-

[7]Annual Report, 1946, pp. 188-89.
[8]*Saturday Evening Post,* October 4, 1947, p. 172.

tration that our foreign policy had last been conducted in behalf of peace and in the true public interest of the United States rather than in behalf of some political party, foreign government, or dubious ideology. One of the most competent of American specialists in diplomatic history had consented to undertake the project, and he was a man not previously identified in any way with revisionist writing. My request was for exactly one thirtieth of the grant allotted for the Langer-Gleason book. The application was turned down by Mr. Zurcher with the summary statement: "I regret that we are unable to supply the funds which you requested for Professor ———'s study." He even discouraged my suggestion that he discuss the idea in a brief conference with the professor in question.

A state of abject terror and intimidation exists among the majority of profesional American historians whose views accord with the facts on the question of responsibility for the Second World War. Several leading historians and publicists who have read my brochure on *The Struggle Against the Historical Blackout* have written me stating that, on the basis of their own personal experience, it is an understatement of the facts. Yet the majority of those historians to whom it has been sent privately have feared even to acknowledge that they have received it or possess it. Only a handful have dared to express approval and encouragement. It is no exaggeration to say that the American Smearbund, operating through newspaper editors and columnists, "hatchetmen" book reviewers, radio commentators, pressure-group intrigue and espionage, and academic pressures and fears, has accomplished about as much in the way of intimidating honest intellectuals in this country as Hitler, Goebbels, Himmler, the Gestapo, and concentration camps were able to do in Nazi Germany.[9]

The mental stalemate produced by this state of mind is well illustrated in the review by Professor Fred Harvey Harrington of Professor Charles C. Tansill's *Back Door to War* in the *Political Science Quarterly*, December 1952. Harrington, in private a moderate revisionist, goes so far as to state that there is "no documentation" for Professor Tansill's statement that the "main objective in American foreign policy since 1900 has been the preservation of

---

[9]The best account of the American Smearbund and its activities is contained in John T. Flynn's brochure, *The Smear Terror,* privately printed, New York, 1948.

the British Empire." This may be compared with the appraisal of the book by a resolute and unafraid revisionist, the eminent scholar Professor George A. Lundberg, who, in a review in *Social Forces*, April 1953, said with regard to the above contention by Tansill: "This thesis is documented to the hilt in almost 700 large pages."

Moreover, the gullibility of many "educated" Americans has been as notable as the mendacity of the "educators." In Communist Russia and Nazi Germany, as well as in Fascist Italy, and in China, the tyrannical rulers found it necessary to suppress all opposition thought in order to induce the majority of the people to accept the material fed them by official propaganda. But, in the United States, with almost complete freedom of the press, speech, and information down to the end of 1941, great numbers of Americans followed the official propaganda line with no compulsion whatever. This is a remarkable and ominous contrast, especially significant because it has been the "educated" element which has been most gullible in accepting official mythology, taking the population as a whole. And this situation has continued since 1945, though of course the public has been less able to get the truth from the avenues of information since V-J Day than it was before Pearl Harbor.

The opposition to revisionism—that is, to truth in the premises —stems in part from emotional fixation on the mythology built up after 1937 and in part from personal loyalty to President Roosevelt and the naturally resulting desire to preserve the impeccability of the Roosevelt legend. In regard to the latter, the Roosevelt adulators are much more solicitous about defending their late chief's foreign policy than they are in upholding the infallibility of his much more creditable domestic program. There is, of course, a powerful vested political interest in perpetuating the accepted mythology about the causes, issues, and results of the Second World War, for much of the public policy of the victorious United Nations since 1945 can only make sense and be justified on the basis of this mythology.

In the United States it was made the ideological basis of the political strategy of the Democratic party and the main political instrument by which it maintained itself in power until 1953. It has also been accepted by many outstanding leaders of the opposition party. It has been indispensable in arousing support for the economic policies which have been used to ward off a depression, with its probably disastrous political reverberations. The eminent railroad executive and astute commentator on world affairs, Robert R. Young, has stated the facts here with realistic clarity in the *Commercial and Financial Chronicle:*

> The clash between a foreign policy which makes sense to Americans and a foreign policy which makes sense to those who seek to perpetuate political office (patronage or prominence) is one which will only be resolved by prohibiting reelection. We are very naive when we describe American foreign policy of recent years as stupid. Indeed, that foreign policy has accomplished its object for it has kept in power (patronage and prominence), election after election, those who conceived and facilitated it.

Powerful pressure groups have also found the mythology helpful in diverting attention from their own role in national and world calamity.

In addition to the opposition of public groups to the truth about responsibility for the Second World War, many historians and other social scientists have a strong professional and personal interest in perpetuating the prewar and wartime mythology. One reason why numerous historians opposed the truth relative to responsibility for the First World War and the main issues therein was that so many of them had taken an active part in spreading the wartime propaganda and had also worked for Colonel House's committee in preparing material for the peacemaking. A considerable number of them went to Paris with President Wilson on his ill-fated adventure. Naturally they were loath to admit that the enterprise in which they had played so prominent a part had proved to be both a fraud and a failure.

Today this situation has been multiplied many fold. Historians and other social scientists veritably swarmed into the various wartime agencies after 1941, especially the Office of War Information and the Office of Strategic Services. They were intimately associated with the war effort and with the shaping of public opinion to conform to the thesis of the pure and limpid idealism and ethereal innocence of the United States and our exclusive devotion to self-defense and world betterment through the sword. Hence, the opposition of historians and social scientists to truth about the responsibility for the Second World War and its obvious results is many times greater than it was in the years following the close of the First World War. Since the war several corps of court historians have volunteered to work to continue the elaboration of official mythology. In addition, the State Department and the Army and Navy have a great swarm of historians dedicated to presenting history as their employers wish it to be written, and at the present time there is a new influx of American historians and social scientists into our "Ministry of Truth."[10]

How the Historical Blackout Operates

The methods followed by the various groups interested in blacking out the truth about world affairs since 1932 are numerous and ingenious, but, aside from subterranean persecution of individuals, they fall mainly into the following patterns or categories: (1) excluding scholars suspected of revisionist views from access to public documents which are freely opened to "court historians" and other apologists for the foreign policy of President Roosevelt; (2) intimidating publishers of books and periodicals, so that even those who might wish to publish books and articles setting forth the revisionist point of view do not dare to do so; (3) ignoring or obscuring published material which embodies revisionist facts and arguments; and (4) smearing revisionist authors and their books.

Denying access to public documents

There is a determined effort to block those suspected of seeking the truth from having access to official documents, other than those which have become public property. The outstanding official and court historians, such as Samuel Eliot Morison, William L. Langer, Herbert Feis, and the like, are given free access to the official archives. Only such things as the most extreme top secrets, like the so-called Kent Documents and President Roosevelt's communications with King George VI, carefully guarded at Hyde Park, are denied to them. Otherwise, they have freedom of access to official documents and the important private diaries of leading public officials.

[10]See below, pp. 128 ff. One of the most conspicuous examples of the entry of historians and other social scientists into the "Ministry of Truth" is afforded by the program and work of the Rand Corporation. See *Fortune,* March 1951, pp. 99–102, 144. See also, *American Historical Review,* April 1953, pp. 761–62.

Many of these important sources are, however, completely sealed off from any historian who is suspected of desiring to ascertain the full and unbiased truth with respect to American foreign policy since 1933. The man who is probably the outstanding scholarly authority on American diplomatic history found himself barred from many of the more important documents. Moreover, many of the notes which he had taken down from those documents he had been permitted to examine were later confiscated by State Department officials.

If the complete official documents would support the generally accepted views with respect to the causes and issues of the war, there would seem to be no reasonable objection to allowing any reputable historian to have free and unimpeded access to such materials. As Charles Austin Beard concisely stated the matter, "Official archives must be open to all citizens on equal terms, with special privileges for none; inquiries must be wide and deep as well as uncensored; and the competition of ideas in the forum of public opinion must be free from political interests or restraints."[11]

The importance of freedom of the archives to writers of sound historical material has also been commented upon by the editor of the London *Times Literary Supplement* of April 18, 1952, in relation to the appearance of Professors William L. Langer and S. E. Gleason's *The Struggle Against Isolation, 1937–1940,* which was produced by the Rockefeller Foundation subsidy mentioned above:

> Once the principle is accepted that governments grant access to their archives to certain chosen historians and refuse it to others, it would be unrealistic to ignore the temptation that may arise in the future to let the choice fall on historians who are most likely to share the official view of the moment and to yield readily to discreet official promptings as to what is suitable, and what is unsuitable, for publication. When this happens, the last barrier on the road to "official history" will have fallen.

Difficulties in publishing revisionist materials

Some might sense that there is a seeming inconsistency between the statement that there has been an attempt to black out revisionism after the Second World War and the undoubted fact that important revisionist books have appeared sooner and in greater

[11]*Saturday Evening Post, loc. cit.*

number since the Second World War than they did after 1918. This gratifying situation in no way contradicts what has been said above relative to the far more vigorous opposition to revisionism since 1945. Nearly all publishers were happy to publish revisionist volumes after 1918, or at least after 1923. But not a single major publisher has issued a revisionist book since 1945; neither is there any evidence that one will do so for years to come. Had not Charles Austin Beard possessed a devoted friend in Eugene Davidson of the Yale University Press, and had not the firms of Henry Regnery and Devin-Adair been in existence, it is very likely that not one revisionist book would have come from the press following V-J Day. For not only are historians who seek to establish the truth prevented from getting much of the material which they need, they also find it very difficult to secure the publication of books embodying such of the truth as they have been able to assemble from the accessible documents.

It would, naturally, be assumed that the first book to give the full inside information on the attack at Pearl Harbor would have been an exciting publishing adventure and that the manuscript would have been eagerly sought after by any and all book-publishing firms. Such, however, was far from the facts. After canvassing the publishing opportunities, George Morgenstern found that the Devin-Adair Company was the only one which had the courage to bring out his brilliant book, *Pearl Harbor: The Story of the Secret War*, in 1947.[12]

Charles Austin Beard informed me that he was so convinced that none of his former commercial publishers would print his critical account of the Roosevelt foreign policy[13] that he did not regard it as even worth while to inquire. He was fortunate enough to have a courageous friend who was head of one of the most important university presses in the country.

The fourth important revisionist book to push its way through the blackout ramparts was William Henry Chamberlin's *America's Second Crusade*.[14] The history of the publication difficulties in connection with the book showed that, in the publishing world,

[12]New York: Devin-Adair Company, 1947.

[13]C. A. Beard, *American Foreign Policy in the Making, 1932–1940* (New Haven, Conn.: Yale University Press, 1946); *President Roosevelt and the Coming of the War, 1941* (New Haven, Conn.: Yale University Press, 1948).

[14]Chicago: Henry Regnery Company, 1950.

there was no more inclination in 1950 than there had been previously to welcome the truth with respect to President Roosevelt's foreign policy and the Second World War.

Chamberlin is a distinguished author. He has written many important books and they have been published by leading publishing houses. But none of his former commercial publishers was interested in the manuscript, though it is probably the most timely and important work Chamberlin has written. The head of one large publishing house, himself a noted publicist, declared his deep personal interest in the book but stated that he did not feel it ethical to jeopardize the financial interests of his company through risking retaliation from the blackout contingent. Two university presses turned down the manuscript, though in each case the director attested to the great merit of the book. That it was finally brought out was due to the courage and public spirit of Henry Regnery, who has published more realistic books relative to the Second World War than all other American publishers combined. Yet Chamberlin's work is neither sensational nor extreme. It is no more than an honest and actually restrained statement of the facts that every American citizen needs to have at hand if we are to avoid involvement in a devastating, fatal "third crusade."

A fifth revisionist book, *Design for War*, by an eminent New York attorney and expert on international law, Frederic R. Sanborn, appeared early in 1951. It was published by the Devin-Adair Company which brought out Mr. Morgenstern's volume.

The sixth and definitive revisionist volume, Professor Charles Callan Tansill's *Back Door to War: The Roosevelt Foreign Policy, 1933–1941*, was published by Regnery. Professor Tansill's previous publishers were not interested in the book.

In a trenchant article on "A Case History in Book Publishing," in the *American Quarterly*, Winter 1949, the distinguished university press editor W. T. Couch tells of the difficulties met with in inducing commercial publishers to print revisionist books, and he goes into detail about the problems encountered in securing a publisher for A. Frank Reel's courageous book *The Case of General Yamashita*.

As a matter of fact, only two small publishing houses in the United States—the Henry Regnery Company and the Devin-Adair Company—have shown any consistent willingess to publish books which frankly aim to tell the truth with respect to the causes and issues of the Second World War. Leading members of two of the largest publishing houses in the country have told me that, whatever their personal wishes in the circumstances, they would not feel it ethical to endanger their business and the property rights of their stockholders by publishing critical books relative to American foreign policy since 1933. And there is good reason for this hesitancy. The book clubs and the main sales outlets for books are controlled by powerful pressure groups which are opposed to truth on such matters. These outlets not only refuse to market critical books in this field but also threaten to boycott other books by those publishers who defy their blackout ultimatum.

When such critical books do get into the bookstores, the sales department frequently refuses to display or promote them. It required the personal intervention of the head of America's largest retail store to insure that one of the leading critical volumes was displayed upon the counter of the book department of the store. In the *American Legion Monthly*, February 1951, Irene Kuhn revealed the efforts of many bookstores to discourage the buying of books critical of administration foreign policy. A striking example of how blackout pressures are able to discourage the sale of revisionist books is the experience at Macy's, in New York City, with the Chamberlin book. Macy's ordered fifty copies and returned forty as unsold. If the book could have been distributed on its merits, Macy's would certainly have sold several thousand copies.

Not only are private sales discouraged, but equally so are sales to libraries. Mr. Regnery discovered that, six months after its publication, there was not one copy of the Chamberlin book in any of the forty-five branches of the New York City Public Library. Another sampling study of the situation in libraries throughout the country showed that the same situation prevailed in most of the nation's libraries, not only in respect to the Chamberlin book, but also in the case of other revisionist volumes like John T. Flynn's *Roosevelt Myth*.[15] Some of the reasons for this are explained by Oliver Carlson in an article on "Slanted Guide to Library Selections" in *The Freeman*, January 14, 1952. As an example, the most influential librarian in the United States has described George Orwell's *Nineteen Eighty-Four* as "paranoia in literature."

[15]New York: Devin-Adair Company, 1948.

The attempt to suppress or exclude revisionist materials from publication extends beyond the book-publishing trade. Whereas, in the late 1920s and early 1930s, all of the more important periodicals were eager to publish competent revisionist articles by reputable scholars, no leading American magazine will today bring out a frank revisionist article, no matter what the professional distinction of the author. Most of them, indeed, even refuse to review revisionist books. The *Progressive* has been the only American periodical which has, with fair consistency, kept its columns open to such material, and its circulation is very limited.

While the periodicals are closed to neo-revisionist materials, they are, of course, wide open and eager for anything which continues the wartime mythology. If the authors of such mythology did not feel reasonably assured that answers to their articles could not be published, it is unlikely that they would risk printing such amazing whitewash as that by General Sherman Miles on "Pearl Harbor in Retrospect," in the *Atlantic Monthly*, July 1948, and Admiral Samuel Eliot Morison's vehement attack on Charles Austin Beard in the August 1948 issue of the same magazine.

Now, Admiral Morison is an able historian of nautical matters and a charming man personally. But his pretensions to anything like objectivity in weighing responsibility for the Second World War can hardly be sustained. In his foreword to Morison's *Battle of the Atlantic*, the late James Forrestal let the cat out of the bag. He revealed that, as early as 1942, Morison had suggested to President Roosevelt that the right kind of history of naval operations during the war should be written, and modestly offered his "services" to do the job so as to reflect proper credit upon the administration. Roosevelt and Secretary Knox heartily agreed to this proposition and Morison was given a commission as captain in the Naval Reserve to write the official history of naval operations in the Second World War.

If Roosevelt and Knox were alive today, they would have no reason to regret their choice of an historian. But, as a "court historian" and "hired man," however able, of Roosevelt and Knox, Admiral Morison's qualifications to take a bow to von Ranke and pass stern judgment on the work of Beard, whom no administration or party was ever able to buy, are not convincing. President Truman's announcement in the newspapers on January 14, 1951, indicated that Morison's services have been recognized and that he is apparently to be court-historian-in-chief during the opening phases of our official entry into the "Nineteen Eighty-Four" system.[16] But Morison's various attacks on Beard were handled with appropriate severity by Professor Howard K. Beale in his address before the American Historical Association on December 28, 1952, published in the August 1953 issue of the *Pacific Historical Review*.

Another example of the accessibility of our leading periodicals to antirevisionist materials was the publication of many articles smearing the reputation of Beard at the time of his death, some of the most bitter articles appearing in journals that had earlier regarded Beard as one of their most distinguished and highly welcome contributors.

Equally illustrative of the tendency to welcome any defense of the traditional mythology and exclude contrary opinions was the publication of the somewhat irresponsible article by Arthur M. Schlesinger, Jr., on "Roosevelt and His Detractors" in the June 1950 issue of *Harper's Magazine*. It was, obviously, proper for the editor to publish this article, but not equally defensible was his inability to "find space" for the publication of an answer, even by one of the outstanding contributers to *Harper's*.

Most of the professional historical magazines are as completely closed to the truth concerning the responsibility for and merits of the Second World War, as are the popular periodicals. Likewise, the great majority of our newspapers are highly hostile to material questioning the traditional mythology about the causes and results of this war. The aversion of the *New York Times* to the truth about Pearl Harbor ten years later is dealt with below.

Ignoring or obscuring revisionist books

In case a revisonist book squeezes through the publishing blackout, almost invariably as a result of the courage of the two small publishing companies mentioned above, the blackout strategists are well prepared to circumvent the possibility of its gaining any wide circulation or popular acceptance. The most common procedure is to accord such books the silent treatment, namely, to refuse to review them at all. As one powerful pressure group has

[16]Morison has recently been promoted to the rank of admiral, thus arriving at the official stature of the famous Alfred T. Mahan.

pointed out, this is the most effective way of nullifying the potential influence of any book. Even highly hostile and critical reviews attract attention to a book and may arouse controversy which will further publicize it. The silent treatment assures a stillbirth to virtually any volume. The late Oswald Garrison Villard recounts his own personal experience with the silent-treatment strategy of editors today:

"I myself rang up a magazine which some months previously had asked me to review a book for them and asked if they would accept another review from me. The answer was 'yes, of course. What book had you in mind?' I replied, 'Morgenstern's *Pearl Harbor*.'

" 'Oh, that's that new book attacking F.D.R. and the war, isn't it?'

" 'Yes.'

" 'Well, how do you stand on it?'

" 'I believe, since his book is based on the records of the Pearl Harbor inquiry, he is right.'

" 'Oh, we don't handle books of that type. It is against our policy to do so.' "

The Henry Regnery Company of Chicago has been more courageous and prolific in the publication of substantial revisionist books than any other concern here or abroad.[17] It has brought out such important books as Leonard von Muralt's *From Versailles to Potsdam*; Hans Rothfels's *German Opposition to Hitler*; Victor Gollancz's *In Darkest Germany*; Freda Utley's *High Cost of Vengeance*; Montgomery Belgion's *Victor's Justice*; Lord Hankey's *Politics: Trials and Errors*; William Henry Chamberlin's *America's Second Crusade*; and Charles Callan Tansill's *Back Door to War*. Mr. Regnery has shown me a careful survey of the treatment accorded these books by our leading newspapers and periodicals. Some have not been reviewed at all; most of them were reviewed sparingly. Almost invariably, when they have been noticed, they have been attacked with great ferocity and uniform unfairness.

The obscuring of the neo-revisionist material may further be illustrated by the space and position assigned to the reviews of

---

17For Mr. Regnery's account of the reception and treatment of these books, see his "A Letter to the Editor of the *Publisher's Weekly*," February 19, 1951.

Beard's *American Foreign Policy in the Making, 1932–1940,* and Morgenstern's *Pearl Harbor* in the *American Historical Review* and in other leading newspapers and periodicals.

Despite the revolutionary nature and vast importance of the Beard book, it was given only a page in the *American Historical Review,* but, amusingly enough, the reviewer used the brief space at his disposal to praise the book. This was not allowed to happen again. Though Morgenstern's book was perhaps the most important single volume published in the field of American history in the year 1947, it was relegated to a book note in the *American Historical Review* and was roundly smeared.

Of all the book-reviewing columnists in New York City papers, only one reviewed Morgenstern's book and he smeared it. The *Saturday Review of Literature* ignored it completely and so did most of the other leading periodicals. Though many infinitely less important books, from the standpoint of timeliness and intrinsic merit of content, received front-page positions therein, neither the Morgenstern book nor the Beard volume was given this place in the Sunday book-review sections of the *New York Times* or *Herald Tribune.* Had these books ardently defended the Roosevelt legend, they would assuredly have been assigned front-page positions. As Oswald Villard remarked of the Beard volume: "Had it been a warm approval of F.D.R. and his war methods, I will wager whatever press standing I have that it would have been featured on the first pages of the *Herald Tribune* 'Books' and the *Times* literary section and received unbounded praise from Walter Millis, Allan Nevins, and other similar axemen."

Mr. Villard's prophecy was vindicated after his death. When the supreme effort to salvage the reputation of Roosevelt and his foreign policy appeared in W. L. Langer and S. E. Gleason's *Challenge to Isolation, 1937–1940,* it was promptly placed on the front page of the *Herald Tribune Book Review* of January 20, 1952, and praised in lavish fashion.

Beard's book on *President Roosevelt and the Coming of the War, 1941,* was so challenging that it could not be ignored. But it did not gain front-page position in either the *New York Times* or the *Herald Tribune.* Though reviewed in a number of newspapers and periodicals, the majority of the reviewers sought to discredit the book rather than to examine its facts and arguments in a spirit of fairness and integrity.

Chamberlin's *America's Second Crusade* was nowhere near as widely reviewed as the significance of the content of the book merited, irrespective of whether or not one agreed with all of the author's conclusions. It was the first comprehensive and critical appraisal of the nature and results of the most momentous project in which the United States was ever involved, politically, economically, or militarily. Hence, it merited careful and extended examination by every newspaper and periodical in the land. But it was reviewed in only a fraction of the leading newspapers, while most of the important periodicals, including the *American Historical Review*, ignored it entirely. In the 1920s periodicals like the *New Republic* and the *Nation* would have reviewed a book of this type lyrically and at great length, and, in all probability, have published special articles and editorials praising it warmly. Most reviews which the Chamberlin book received were of the smearing variety. The *New York Times* and *Herald Tribune* both reviewed the book in hostile fashion, gave it very brief reviews, and placed these in an obscure position.

Frederic R. Sanborn's able and devastating *Design for War* received about the same treatment as the Chamberlin volume. It was ignored by the great majority of the newspapers and by virtually all the important periodicals. The *New York Times* reviewed the book rather promptly, if not conspicuously, but handed it over to their leading academic hatchet man, Samuel Flagg Bemis. Though prodded by Sanborn, the *Herald Tribune* delayed the review from March to August and then assigned it to Gordon A. Craig, a leading antirevisionist among the historians frequently employed by the *Times* and *Herald Tribune* in attacking books critical of Roosevelt foreign policy. Sanborn's book was not reviewed at all by *Time*, *Newsweek*, the *New Yorker*, the *Nation*, the *New Republic*, *Harper's*, the *Atlantic Monthly*, or the *Saturday Review of Literature*, though Sanborn wrote letters of inquiry to all of them. Correspondence with the *Saturday Review of Literature* from April to the end of September failed to produce a review. If a comparable book had appeared at any time between 1923 and 1935, there is every reason to believe that the *Nation* and *New Republic*, for example, would have hailed it with near-hysterical joy and given excessive space to praising and promoting it. The *American Historical Review* did not review or even notice the Sanborn volume.

So far as can be ascertained at the time these lines are revised [December 1952], Charles Callin Tansill's *Back Door to War* was treated by the press in essentially the same manner as it had handled the Chamberlin and Sanborn volumes, although it is the definitive revisionist contribution and deserves as much consideration as Sidney B. Fay's *Origins of the World War* received in 1928.

It received slightly more attention than did Chamberlin and Sanborn in the newspapers, perhaps because a determined effort was made to get the book into the hands of the editor of every important newspaper in the country. The majority of the newspaper reviews were of a smearing nature. As one example of such a review by an interventionist newspaper, we may cite the following from the *San Francisco Chronicle* of July 27, 1952: "To bring forth a very small mouse, Professor Tansill has labored mountainously to assemble this helter-skelter collection of facts, documents and hearsay about America's prewar foreign policy.... This book is not history. It is awkward special pleading." The author of the review hid behind the initials "M.S."

The book failed to make the front page of either the *New York Times Book Review* or of the *New York Herald Tribune Book Review*. It was reviewed on page 3 of the former (May 11, 1952) and on page 10 of the latter (June 1, 1952), rather briefly in both cases. Even so, Dexter Perkins, who reviewed the book for the *Times*, had to request twice the space originally assigned. Among the important periodicals only the *Freeman*, the *Saturday Review of Literature*, and the *Nation* reviewed the book, the latter two rather belatedly. *Time*, *Newsweek*, the *Atlantic*, and *Harper's* gave the volume the "silent treatment," ignoring it entirely. The editor of the *New Republic* treated the book to an almost obscene smear. In the 1920s all of these periodicals (which were then in existence) would have reviewed the book promptly and at length, and it would have evoked almost frenzied ecstacy on the part of the *Nation* and *New Republic*.

The jaundiced and biased attitude of periodicals in reviewing or ignoring such books as these was well revealed at the time of the appearance of the ardently pro-Roosevelt masterpiece by W. L. Langer and S. E. Gleason, *Challenge to Isolation, 1937–1940*. In this instance virtually all of the magazines which had ignored the books by Morgenstern, Chamberlin, Sanborn, and Tansill immediately rushed into print with prominent and lyrical reviews of the

Langer-Gleason volume. Among all the editors of professional journals in the historical and social science field, only Professor Howard W. Odum, editor of *Social Forces*, has been willing to open his publication to full and fair reviewing of revisionist volumes.

One of the most impressive examples of the ignoring and obscuring of the writings of men critical of our foreign policy since 1937 is presented by the case of Francis Neilson. Mr. Neilson is a distinguished publicist and he served as a member of Parliament before he came to the United States. He was the principal "angel" of the original *Freeman* and, like John T. Flynn, was once a darling of American liberals who were, in those days, revisionists and anti-interventionists. Mr. Neilson's *How Diplomats Make War* (1915) was the first revisionist volume to be published on the First World War, and it is still read with respect.

When Mr. Neilson opposed our interventionism after 1937, his erstwhile liberal friends fell away from him. Being a man of means, he was able to publish his gigantic five-volume work, *The Tragedy of Europe*, privately. It was scarcely noticed in any review, though it was praised by no less a personage than President Robert Maynard Hutchins of the University of Chicago. In 1950 Mr. Neilson published, again privately, a condensation of the more vital portions of his larger work, entitling it *The Makers of War*. The book contains a great amount of valuable revisionist material not embodied in any other revisionist volume on the Second World War. But, Mr. Neilson assured me personally, it has never been reviewed at all.

Smearing revisionist books

When, rather rarely and for one reason or another, a newspaper or a periodical decides actually to review a revisionist book rather than to accord it the silent treatment, it has available a large supply of hatchet men who can be relied upon to attack and smear revisionist volumes and to eulogize the work of court historians and others who seek to perpetuate the traditional mythology.[18] For example, the *New York Times* has its own staff of such hatch-

---

[18]See the brochure by Dr. John H. Sachs, *Hatchet Men* (New Oxford, Pa., privately printed, 1947); and Oswald Garrison Villard, "Book-Burning—U.S. Style," *The Progressive*, April 28, 1947.

et men, among them Otto D. Tolischus, Charles Poore, Orville Prescott, Karl Schriftgiesser, Drew Middleton, and others. When these do not suffice, it can call upon academicians of similar inclination, such as Arthur M. Schlesinger, Jr., Allan Nevins, Henry Steele Commager, Gordon A. Craig, Samuel Flagg Bemis, Dexter Perkins, and others. The *Herald Tribune* has Walter Millis, August Heckscher, and their associates on its staff, and also turns to such academicians as those mentioned above, whose gifts and talents are not limited to the *Times*.

The smearing device used almost universally in discrediting neo-revisionist books is a carry-over of the propaganda strategy perfected by Charles Michelson in political technique, and extended by Joseph Goebbels, John Roy Carlson, and others, namely, seeking to destroy the reputation of an opponent by associating him, however unfairly, with some odious quality, attitude, policy, or personality, even though this may have nothing to do with the vital facts in the situation. It is only a complex and skillful application of the old adage about "giving a dog a bad name." This is an easy and facile procedure, for it all too often effectively disposes of an opponent without involving the onerous responsibility of facing the facts.[19] The "blackout boys" have even implied that the effort to tell the truth about responsibility for the Second World War is downright wicked. Samuel Flagg Bemis declares that such an excursion into intellectual integrity is "serious, unfortunate, deplorable."[20]

Inasmuch as the Morgenstern book was the first to shake the foundations of the interventionist wartime propaganda and because Morgenstern is not a professional historian of longtime standing, his work was greeted with an avalanche of smears. Virtually the only fair reviews of the Morgenstern volume were those by Edwin M. Borchard, George A. Lundberg, Harry Paxton Howard, and Admiral H. E. Yarnell. There was rarely any effort whatever to wrestle with the vast array of facts and documentary evidence which, both Beard and Admiral Yarnell maintained, bore out all of Morgenstern's essential statements and conclusions. Rather, he was greeted with an almost unrelieved volley of smears.

[19]See Towner Phelan, "Modern School for Scandal," *The Freeman*, September 24, 1951, pp. 813–17.
[20]*Journal of Modern History*, XIX (March, 1947), 55–59.

Some reviewers rested content with pointing out that Morgenstern is a young man and, hence, cannot be supposed to know much, even though the *New York Times* handed over to Arthur M. Schlesinger, Jr., a younger man, the responsibility for reviewing Beard's great book on *President Roosevelt and the Coming of the War, 1941.* Another reviewer asserted that all that needed to be said to refute and silence the book was to point out that Morgenstern is employed by the *Chicago Tribune.* Others stressed the fact that he is only an amateur, dabbling with documents, without the training afforded by the graduate historical seminar, though Morgenstern was an honor student of history at the University of Chicago. It was apparent to unbiased readers that most of the professors who reviewed his book departed entirely from any seminar canons of research and criticism which they may have earlier mastered. Morgenstern surely worked and wrote in closer conformity to von Ranke's exhortations than his professorial reviewers.

Other reviewers sought to dispose of the Morgenstern book by stating that it was "bitterly partisan," was composed in a state of "blind anger," or written with "unusual asperity," though it is actually the fact that Morgenstern is far less bitter, angry, or blind than his reviewers. Indeed, the tone of his book is more one of urbane satire than of indignation. Few books of this type have been freer of any taint of wrath and fury. The attitude of such reviewers is a good example of what the psychologists call the mechanism of "projection." The reviewers attributed to Morgenstern the "blind anger" that they themselves felt when compelled to face the truth.

In reviewing the book for the *Infantry Journal,* May 1947, Harvey A. DeWeerd declared that it was "the most flagrant example of slanted history" that had come to his attention "in recent years," but he failed to make it clear that the uniqueness in the slanting of Morgenstern's book was that it was "slanted" toward the truth, something which was, and still is, quite unusual in historical writing on this theme. Probably the most complete smearing of the Morgenstern book was performed by Walter Millis in the *Herald Tribune Book Review*, February 9, 1947, though, with all the extensive space at his disposal, he made no serious effort to come to grips with the facts in the situation. He merely elaborated the smear in the caption: "Twisting the Pearl Harbor Story: A Documented Brief for a Highly Biased, Bitter, Cynical View."

Gordon A. Craig, of Princeton, reviewing the book in the *New York Times*, February 9, 1947, rested content with stating that the book was no more than anti-Roosevelt "mythology" and completely "unbelievable," though he adduced no relevant evidence in support of these assertions.

One of the most remarkable attacks on the book was made by a onetime ardent revisionist historian, Oron J. Hale, in the *Annals of the American Academy*, July 1947. After first assailing the book with the charge of bitter partisanship and asserting that the author made only a fake "parade" of the "externals of scholarship," Hale sought manfully but futilely to find serious errors in Morgenstern's materials. He then concluded that all or most of the statements in the book were true but that the book as a whole was a "great untruth." This reverses the usual line of the current apologists for the Roosevelt foreign policy, like Thomas A. Bailey and Arthur M. Schlesinger, Jr., who now agree that most of Roosevelt's public statements thereupon were untrue but that his program as a whole was a great truth which exemplified the desirable procedure of the "good officer"—the conscientious public servant.

The fact that Morgenstern is an editorial writer for the *Chicago Tribune* and that the *Tribune* has opened its columns to revisionist writings has encouraged the Smearbund to seek to identify revisionism and all revisionist writers with the *Tribune*. Even Beard's books were charged with being dominated by the *Tribune* policy. Only recently a reviewer in the *New Yorker* linked Beard and the *Tribune* and referred to the "Charles Austin Beard-*Chicago Tribune*" view of war origins. Max Lerner wrote that "the man who once mercilessly flayed Hearst became the darling of McCormick."

No phase of the smear campaign could well be more preposterous. Aside from being willing to accept the truth relative to Roosevelt foreign policy, Beard and the *Tribune* had little in common. The American Civil Liberties Union once warmly praised Colonel McCormick for his valiant battle against the Minnesota press gag law. There was no attempt, then, to link the Civil Liberties Union with the total editorial policy of the *Tribune*. Roger Baldwin was not portrayed as a tool of Colonel McCormick, nor was there any hint of a Civil Liberties Union–McCormick axis. Those who write in behalf of freedom of the press can always gain access to the columns of the *Chicago Tribune*, but there is no thought in such cases of linking them with the total editorial policy of the *Tribune*.

Due to the fact that Beard was a trained and venerable scholar and, hence, obviously not a juvenile amateur in using historical documents, that he had a worldwide reputation as one of the most eminent and productive historians and political scientists the United States has ever produced, that he had served as president of the American Political Science Association and of the American Historical Association, and that he was awarded, in 1948, the Gold Medal of the National Institute of Arts and Letters for the best historical work of the preceding decade, it required more than usual gall and trepidation to apply the smear technique to Beard and his two splendid books on American foreign policy.

Yet Beard did not escape unscathed, though his facts and objectivity cannot be validly challenged. As Louis Martin Sears pointed out in the *American Historical Review*: "The volume under review is said to give annoyance to the followers of Franklin Delano Roosevelt. If that be true, their faith is scarcely founded upon a rock, for no more objective treatment could readily be conceived. The author nowhere injects a personal opinion."[21] Any testimonials as to Beard's historical prowess are, invariably, a red flag to the Smearbund bull. Only this consideration makes such things as Lewis Mumford's resignation from the National Institute of Arts and Letters, because of the award of the above-mentioned medal to Beard, or Harry D. Gideonse's explosion in the *New Leader*,[22] at all explicable.

The difficulty of attacking Beard relative to his status as an historian diverted most of the smearing of him into the allegation that his work is invalidated and unreliable because he was an "isolationist." The absurdity of this charge is obvious. Beard did, from 1937 onward, courageously and sanely warn against the manner in which the Roosevelt policies were deliberately leading us into a foreign war against the will of the overwhelming mass of the American people in what was supposed to be a democratic system of government. Beard's stand may not have been wise, though the facts today overwhelmingly prove its soundness, but such an attitude has nothing whatever to do with any literal isolationism unless one defines internationalism as chronic meddling

[21]April, 1947, p. 532.
[22]June 12, 1948.

abroad and unwavering support of our entry into any extant foreign war.

Any attempt to brand Beard as a literal isolationist is, of course, completely preposterous. Few men have had a wider international perspective or experience. In his early academic days he helped to found Ruskin College, Oxford. He had travelled, advised, and been held in high esteem from Tokyo to Belgrade.

The irresponsibility of this form of smearing Beard is well illustrated by the innuendo of Samuel Eliot Morison and Perry Miller that Beard was an ignorant isolationist with an archaic and naive view of world affairs because he was deaf and lived on a farm with his cows, thus implying that he had shut himself off from the world and human associations and did not know what was going on about him. That such charges were utterly without foundation is well known to anybody with any knowledge whatever of Beard and his mode of life and must have been known to be untrue by Admiral Morison and Professor Miller themselves.

Beard provided himself with a most efficient hearing instrument which enabled him to carry on personal conversations with the utmost facility. He probably enjoyed wider personal contact with scholars and publicists than any other American historian down to the day of his death. He was visited at his suburban home constantly by a stream of prominent academic and scholarly admirers. He travelled widely and spent his winters in North Carolina. His deafness did not affect his personal relations or scholarly interests and activities in the slightest. His mode of life, at the most, only gave him the occasional quiet and detachment needed to digest and interpret the mass of information which came to him as a result of his wide reading and his extensive personal contacts with American and foreign scholars, both young and old. His dairy farm was located some twenty miles from his home.

I was present a few years ago at a conference on foreign affairs attended by about forty leading savants. Most of them wrung their hands about the sorry state of the world today, but only two or three were frank and candid enough to discern and admit that the majority of the conditions which they were so dolorously deploring stemmed directly from the foreign policies of Franklin D. Roosevelt, from his Chicago bridge speech of October 1937, to the Yalta Conference of early 1945. Beard was assailed for his "isolationism" and "cultural lag" by both the chairman and the chief participant for no earthly reason save that he opposed the policies which had led to the chaos over which the conference was holding the coroner's inquest—but with no intention of declaring it a homicide or seeking the culprit. They vented their spleen on a man who had advised against risking the ambuscade which led to the murder.

It is both vicious and silly to brand a person an "isolationist" merely because he opposed our entry into the Second World War. Personally, I opposed our entry with all the energy and power at my command—just as vigorously as did Beard. But it also happens that I wrote one of the longest chapters in the first important book ever published in behalf of the League of Nations and that I have ever since supported any move or policy which seemed to me likely to promote international good will and world peace. Sane internationalism is one thing; it is something quite different to support our entry into a war likely to ruin civilization mainly to promote the political prospects of a domestic leader, however colorful and popular, to satisfy the neurotic compulsions of special interests and pressure groups, and to pull the chestnuts of foreign nations out of the fire.

The whole issue of "isolationism" and the epithet "isolationist" has been a very effective phase of the smearing technique invented and applied by interventionists between 1937 and Pearl Harbor, and so naively exposed and betrayed by Walter Johnson in his book *The Battle Against Isolation*. The absurd character of the whole process of smearing by the method of alleging "isolationism" has been devastatingly revealed by George A. Lundberg in his article on "Semantics in International Relations" in the *American Perspective*.[24] Senator Taft put the matter in a nutshell when he asserted that to call any responsible person an isolationist today is nothing less than idiocy—one might add, malicious idiocy.

The only man of any intellectual importance who ever believed in isolationism was a German economist, Johann Heinrich von Thünen (1783–1850), author of *The Isolated State* (1826), and he espoused the idea only to provide the basis for formulating eco-

[23]Chicago: University of Chicago Press, 1944. For a corrective, see Wayne S. Cole, *America First: The Battle Against Intervention, 1940-1941* (Madison: University of Wisconsin Press, 1953).
[24]June, 1948, pp. 127-32.

nomic abstractions. In short, isolationism is no more than a semantic smear fiction invented by globaloney addicts.

Governor Adlai E. Stevenson of Illinois is reported to have said in a commencement address in June 1952 that "isolationism has not lost all of its emotional appeal, but it has lost its intellectual respectability." Unless one is willing to lapse completely into "Nineteen Eighty-Four" doublethink, it would seem that exactly the opposite is the truth. From Woodrow Wilson's war address on April 6, 1917, to President Truman's denunciation of cuts in the 1952 European aid allotment, interventionism has rested entirely on propaganda and emotional appeals. It has never been able to stand for a moment on the ground of empiricism, logic, and fact. If results are any test of the validity of a position, no program in human history has had less confirmation and vindication than has the intervention of the United States in foreign quarrels. On the other hand, isolationism, which means no more than international sanity and the avoidance of national suicide, has never been able to appeal to war excitement, the propaganda of fear, and other emotional fictions. It has always been compelled to rely upon reason and sanity. It may be that emotionalism is a better guide for public policy than rationality, but to claim that interventionism and globaloney can claim priority in respect to rationality is palpably preposterous.

The internationalists of the earlier era, for whom I wrote and lectured from coast to coast for twenty years after 1918, were true believers in internationalism, good will, and peace, and worked to secure these objectives. The globaloney and interventionist crowd, while prating about internationalism and peace, have done more than anybody else, except the totalitarian dictators, to promote nationalism and to revive and direct the war spirit. They have created an unprecedented spirit of interventionism, militarism, and intolerance in the United States and have helped to provoke a similar development in Soviet Russia. While blatant nationalism was checked temporarily in Germany and Italy, it has been stimulated elsewhere, from England to Indochina, eastern Asia, and South Africa. The United Nations have steadily become more nationalistic and less united, and the world trembles and shivers on the brink of the third world war before the peace treaties have all been negotiated to conclude the second. There is all too much truth in the statement of an eminent publicist that Alger

Hiss's long-continued activities as an aggressive internationalist of the recent vintage did far more harm to the United States than handing over any number of secret State Department documents which he could have transcribed and transmitted to the Russians. The columnist Jay Franklin has given us a good summary picture of the fruits of interventionism by contrasting the twentieth-century American casualty record under five "isolationist" Republican presidents and under three interventionist Democratic presidents:

Republican Presidents	Casualties
Theodore Roosevelt (1901–9)	0
William H. Taft (1909–13)	0
Warren G. Harding (1921–23)	0
Calvin Coolidge (1923–29)	0
Herbert Hoover (1929–33)	0
Total for 24 Republican years	0

Democratic Presidents	Casualties
Woodrow Wilson(1913–21)	364,800
Franklin D. Roosevelt (1933–45)	1,134,527
Harry Truman (1945–53)	129,153
Total for 28 Democratic years	1,628,480

Average U.S. war casualties per Republican year, 0.
Average U.S. war casualties per Democratic year, 58,160.

Though Catholic circles have been unusually fair in tolerating the truth about the causes of the Second World War, the pressure on the editors was so great that even the enlightened *Commonweal* permitted Mason Wade to attack Beard in its columns. But the most irresponsible attempt to attack Beard as an "isolationist" came with almost uniquely bad taste from the pen of Harry D. Gideonse, who reviewed Beard's *President Roosevelt and the Coming of the War, 1941*, in the *New Leader*.[25]

Beard was a native-born American who labored mightily for over fifty years to improve many phases of American intellectual and public life. No American historian, past or present, had a more honorable record as an active and effective intellectual patriot. He had never written a word which placed the interests of

[25] June 12, 1948.

other nations above those of our country. Gideonse, on the other hand, is Dutch-born, surely an honorable paternity. But there is little evidence that he has ever become completely immersed in Americanism or has taken on a thoroughly American point of view. In his public statements over many years he has always given evidence of a robust internationalism which has little primary regard for American institutions or traditions. His internationalism appears to have a twofold basis: a hangover of the Dutch imperialism of the Dutch East India Company tycoons of the seventeenth and eighteenth centuries,[26] and the virus of current American globaloney. Anyhow, it has paid off remarkably well, for Gideonse was summoned from Chicago to Columbia University and then, to the amazement even of his friends, suddenly catapulted into the presidency of Brooklyn College in 1939.

While Gideonse finds other nonfactual grounds for assaulting Beard, he holds that Beard's alleged isolationism is all that is needed to brush the book aside. Indeed, all that is required for that is the fact, as Gideonse tells us twice in the course of his review, that it has been praised as a very great book by the "isolationist" *Chicago Tribune*. It might be cogently observed that the *Tribune* has also praised the Bible, Shakespeare's works, and Einstein's writings on relativity. But Gideonse has not laughed this off yet. If praise by the *Chicago Tribune* were not enough to destroy the validity of Beard's book, then, in Gideonse's view, it would be amply disposed of by the fact that he quotes, even sparingly, statements by eminent "isolationists" like Senators Burton K. Wheeler and Gerald P. Nye. Not even the fact, which Gideonse concedes, that he also cites Eleanor Roosevelt frequently and with respect, could redeem Beard after he had revealed his acquaintance with the statements of allegedly nefarious "isolationist" personalities.

Though, as we have made clear, reviewers have, naturally, been a trifle hesitant in daring to minimize Beard's status as an historian, Walter Millis and Gideonse have not been dismayed or sidetracked even here. In his review of Beard's *President Roosevelt and the Coming of the War, 1941*, in the *Herald Tribune Book Review*,[27] Millis contended that Beard is not entitled to rank as an

[26]On this point, see his letter in the *New York Times*, January 10, 1949.
[27]April 11, 1948.

objective historian according to formal academic fictions, but really belongs back with Tertullian, Orosius, Gregory of Tours, and other "Dark Age" exemplars of the "Devil theory of history."

But it remained for Gideonse to sail in and seek to divest Beard of all claims to any standing as an historical scholar. Just why Gideonse should presume to pass on questions of historiography and to grade historians is not quite evident, though he has been doing so for some years. Professionally, though admittedly a very talented classroom orator and an effective "rabble-rouser" of the student body, he was only a somewhat obscure economist when he strode into Flatbush with his mace. But Gideonse did not hesitate to administer a sharp slap to the members of the American Historical Association, who elected Beard to their presidency in 1933, by pooh-poohing the general scholarly opinion that Beard was the "dean of living American historians." This notion and pretension, says Gideonse, is purely "fictitious." Actually, according to Gideonse, Beard has only been a lifelong pamphleteer, and his books on Roosevelt's foreign policy are cheap journalism.

In the light of all this, one could read with considerable amusement and sardonic humor an announcement in the *New York Times* of September 8, 1948, that Gideonse opened the college year at Flatbush with an address to entering freshmen in which he gravely and sternly asserted that "truthfulness" is a main and indispensable quality of a college teacher; one which does not, perhaps, extend to college presidents.

There were many other attacks on Beard's last two great books. They usually took one of two forms. First, there were efforts to dispose of them by brief, casual Jovian or flippant smears, without giving any attention whatever to the facts or meeting the arguments of the books. Such was Arthur M. Schlesinger, Jr.'s smear in the *Partisan Review*,[28] implying that Beard sought to justify collaboration with the Nazis; Max Lerner's slur to the effect that they were "two rather weird affairs"; Perry Miller's description of them as "two frenetic indictments of Franklin Roosevelt" (implying, if Miller knew the meaning of the words he was using, that Beard must have been insane); and Quincy Wright's even briefer disposition of them as "a strange argument" (strange, presumably, to Wright in that the argument was based on facts).

[28] October, 1949.

The other type of approach has been to smother the book under a vast welter of side issues, non sequiturs, and irrelevant scoldings. This was well illustrated by the procedure of Charles C. Griffin, an expert on Latin American history, who was selected to review Beard's last book for the *American Historical Review*.[29] He buried the book under four and a half pages of impenetrable, irrelevant, and disapproving fog, rarely coming to grips with the essential facts and arguments. About the only fair and scholarly review that the book received was by the chief authority in the field, Charles C. Tansill, in the *Mississippi Valley Historical Review*.[30]

On the occasion of Beard's death one might have supposed that the opportunity would have been taken to pay a tribute to his greatness as a teacher, historian, political scientist, and liberal, at least in those journals to which Beard had been for years one of the most honored contributors, and that there would have been articles by writers who had long been admirers of Beard, until he began to examine Roosevelt's foreign policy. Instead of this we were treated to an obscene performance which reminded fair observers of jackals and hyenas howling about the body of a dead lion. Especially in point were the articles by Max Lerner in the *New Republic*, October 25 and November 1, 1948; by Perry Miller in the *Nation*, September 25, 1948; and by Peter Levin in *Tomorrow*, March 1949.

In these articles most of the smears which had been irresponsibly thrown at Beard during the previous several years were amalgamated and he was portrayed as a senile, embittered, and confused "isolationist" and a traitor to the liberal cause. There was even an effort to undermine confidence in Beard's monumental books which had preceded his volumes on the foreign policy of President Roosevelt. Lerner held up to ridicule Beard's social and civic ideal: "A continental economy, spaciously conceived, controlled in a common-sense way, yielding a gracious life without all the horrors of foreign entanglements." As of 1953, such an ideal might well evoke the heartiest enthusiasm on the part of any thoughtful American. Lerner characterized Roosevelt's foreign policy as a consistent attempt to promote "the collective demo-

[29]January, 1949, pp. 382–86.
[30]December, 1948, pp. 532–534.

cratic will reluctantly having to shape a world in which it could survive.'' How well it succeeded in achieving this result will be apparent from an examination of Chamberlin's *America's Second Crusade*.

The campaign of vilification and distortion against Beard has continued long after his death. One of the most absurd attacks appeared in 1952 in a book by John B. Harrison, a teacher of history at Michigan State College, entitled *This Age of Global Strife*. Harrison writes:

> This prominent historian undertook in the last days of his eccentric old age to prove by ponderous documentation that President Roosevelt set out from the beginning of the war in Europe to stealthily and deceitfully maneuver the United States into a war whose outcome was of no real concern to the American people. It is a deplorable collection of halftruths and distortions. Anyone who reads it should read also Samuel E. Morison's brilliant analysis of it in the *Atlantic Monthly,* August, 1948.

A book containing material of this sort could be published by the old and reputable firm of Lippincott seven years after V-J Day.

The reception accorded Chamberlin's *America's Second Crusade* was in keeping with the blackout procedure and in line with that given to the Morgenstern and Beard volumes. Chamberlin was too important and well-known an author to be given the silent treatment by all newspapers and periodicals, though the leading liberal periodicals tended to ignore his book. It was, naturally, glowingly praised in the *Chicago Tribune* and equally lavishly smeared by the *New York Post*.

The *New York Times* treated the book about as badly as feasible under the circumstances.[31] While it placed a long review of a slight book by the elder Schlesinger on page 3 of the Sunday *Book Review*, it relegated Chamberlin's striking volume to page 34. It chose as the reviewer of the book Samuel Flagg Bemis, well known as perhaps the bitterest critic of revisionist writing among the historians.

But even Bemis was unable to make much headway against Chamberlin's facts and logic. He frankly admitted that he would not ''argue the case with Mr. Chamberlin.'' In reviewing the Morgenstern book, Bemis had written that the American situation in late 1941 constituted ''the most awful danger that ever confronted

[31] *New York Times Book Review,* October 15, 1950, p. 34.

our nation." He still stuck to this thesis, despite his admission that there is no factual basis for it: "That captured Nazi archives do not reveal any actual plans to attack the New World, as Mr. Chamberlin repeatedly stresses, does not make any difference. The intention was there." Bemis pictured Germany and Japan as "the two colossi whose power in victory would have closed on our freedom with the inexorable jaws of a global vise." Therefore, our second crusade was a success and a necessity, even though Bemis admits that Russia is now more powerful than Japan and Germany combined could ever have become, and its power is concentrated in one nation rather than being divided among two, who might often have clashed: "Stalin has stepped into everything that Hitler and Japan first started out to get, and more. Soviet Russia has rolled up an agglomeration of power greater than ever menaced the United States, even in 1941."

Bemis concluded his review with what is possibly the most incredible example of "foot-swallowing" in the whole history of book reviewing:

> One thing ought to be evident to all of us: by our victory over Germany and Japan, no matter what our folly in losing the peace, we have at least survived to confront the second even greater menace of another totalitarian power.... We might not stand vis-a-vis with the Soviets today if President Roosevelt had not entertained a conviction that action against the Axis was necessary.

In other words, all the physical, financial, and moral losses of the United States in the Second World War were justified and well expended in order that we might face another world war against a far stronger enemy. With these comments we may well leave Bemis to the logicians.

The *New York Herald Tribune Book Review* handled the Chamberlin book much as did the *Times*.[32] It placed the review on the twelfth page, following reviews of many relatively trivial volumes. It did not seek out a professional critic, but assigned one of its own "hatchet men," August Heckscher, to write the review. While the book was smeared as a revival of "pre-war isolationism," Heckscher was not able to succeed any better than Bemis in disposing of Chamberlin's material and arguments. He had to rest satisfied with espousing the "perpetual-war-for-perpetual-peace" program of our current internationalists. If the first and second

[32]October 15, 1950, p. 12.

crusades have failed to provide peace, security, and prosperity, we can "keep on trying." Other and more bloody crusades may turn the trick, though even Arnold J. Toynbee has admitted that any further crusades may leave only the pygmies—or, perhaps, only the apes or ants—to wrestle with the aftermath.

Perhaps the most remarkable example of smearing the Chamberlin book was the review which was published in the *New Leader*,[33] written by our old friend, Harry D. Gideonse.

The *New Leader* is a sprightly journal controlled mainly by Socialists and ex-Socialists who deserted Norman Thomas in his brave stand against our entry into the Second World War, and by totalitarian liberals. Both groups were fanatically in favor of our intervention in the Second World War and are now in the vanguard of those who wish us to enter a third crusade in the interest of perpetual war for perpetual peace and the suppression of Red sin throughout the world. Chamberlin writes for this periodical, though his presence seems somewhat incongruous in such an editorial group.

But the fact that Chamberlin is a regular contributor to the *New Leader* weighed less heavily with the editor than his offense in debunking our first and second crusades and his warning against our entering a third. Therefore it was decided that Chamberlin's book must be smeared, and a man was chosen to do it who could be relied upon. There was no doubt about Gideonse's dependability for the task, both from his well-known general attitude toward interventionism and from his earlier elaborate smearing of Beard in the *New Leader*.

Gideonse did not let the editor down, except that he was only able to bring to bear against Chamberlin the same threadbare smears that he had used against Beard. He led off with a blanket condemnation: "This is a bitter and unconvincing book." The worthlessness of much of Chamberlin's book, according to Gideonse, required nothing more in the way of proof than to show that he agreed with Colonel McCormick and the *Chicago Tribune:* "At least half of the contents of Mr. Chamberlin's book is another rehash of the *Chicago Tribune* history of World War II." Gideonse repeated the old alarmist dud to the effect that, if we had not gone to war against Hitler, he would have made a vassal of Stalin and Soviet Russia and would have controlled the Old World "from the English Channel to Vladivostok." In the December 18, 1950, issue of the *New Leader*, Chamberlin submitted a crushing answer to Gideonse and other smearing reviewers.

The *New York Post* called Chamberlin a "totalitarian conservative" and painted him as a special favorite of the McCormick-Patterson axis. The overwhelming majority of the reviews of the book did not rise above the level of smearing, the lowest point of which was reached in the review by James M. Minifie in the *Saturday Review of Literature*.[34]

That the progress of disillusionment with respect to the results of the second crusade and the shock of the Korean War may have made a few editors a trifle more tolerant of reality in world affairs was, possibly, demonstrated by the fact that Chamberlin's book was warmly praised in the review in the *Wall Street Journal* and was accorded fair treatment in the interventionist *Chicago Daily News*.

Frederic R. Sanborn's concise, elaborately documented, and closely reasoned volume, *Design for War*, devoted chiefly to an account of President Roosevelt's secret war program after 1937, was treated much like the Morgenstern and Chamberlin books, though it was more extensively ignored in the press. When not ignored, it was smeared in most of the reviews. The *New York Times* thought that it had taken care of the matter by handing the book over to Samuel Flagg Bemis for reviewing. By this time, however, Bemis had read the latest edition of my *Struggle Against the Historical Blackout*, with its account of his foot-swallowing feat in his *Times* review of the Chamberlin volume. So Bemis, while rejecting Sanborn's version of American diplomacy from 1937 to Pearl Harbor, was relatively cautious and respectful.

Months after the book appeared, the *Herald Tribune* finally and reluctantly reviewed it, after much prodding by Sanborn. It handed it over to another warhorse among the hatchet men, Gordon A. Craig of Princeton. He indulged mainly in the shadow-boxing for which Walter Millis had shown such talent. The review, while of the smearing variety, was evasive, as had been Craig's review of Morgenstern's book in the *Times* years before. He refused to confront the facts and even went so far in historical humor as to accept Cordell Hull's statements at their face value.

[34]November 18, 1950.

The Sanborn book was smeared in most of the Scripps-Howard papers that reviewed it at all (*vide* the *Rocky Mountain News*, February 18, 1951), though this chain had been in the vanguard of prewar "isolationism." A characteristic newspaper slur was that of the *Chattanooga Times*, which proclaimed that the Sanborn book was "as impartial as the *Chicago Tribune* or Westbrook Pegler."

Felix Wittmer reviewed the book in the *New Leader*, March 26, 1951. The editors had, apparently, become bored themselves with the monotonous uniformity of the unvaried dead cats thrown at revisionist books by Harry Gideonse. The Wittmer review was a masterpiece of "doublethink." He smeared the book as "a sad spectacle," and "a biased and myopic account of diplomacy in the guise of objectivity." He accused Sanborn of "amazing ignorance of modern Japanese policies." Yet, a little later on, he expressed himself as in almost complete agreement with Sanborn's account of the crucial Japanese-American negotiations in 1941: "It is perfectly true—as Dr. Sanborn proves—that in 1941 the Japanese seriously wanted peace and that Roosevelt and Hull used every possible device to forestall it, and to provoke an open attack by Japan." He even admits that Roosevelt and Hull anticipated this attack. He excuses all this on the ground that our entry into the war was obligatory for American security from Nazi invasion and for the salvation of humanity, and that the provocation of the Japanese was only "penetrating foresight," because Hitler and Mussolini were just mean enough not to rise to Roosevelt's war bait in the Atlantic. Hence, we had to incite Japan to attack us in order to get into the war through the Pacific back door. Even the *New Leader* felt impelled to publish a rejoinder by Sanborn.

We have already pointed out that virtually all the important periodicals—*Time, Newsweek*, the *New Yorker*, the *Saturday Review of Literature*, the *Nation*, the *New Republic, Harper's*, and the *Atlantic Monthly*—had wisely decided that they could protect the Roosevelt and interventionist legend better by ignoring the book entirely than by smearing it in reviews. The *American Historical Review* did not even mention the volume in a book note.

The reviewing of the book by Charles Callan Tansill, *Back Door to War*, ran true to the form established with reference to revisionist volumes. The Tansill tome is more outspoken and more heavily documented than any other revisionist treatise. So, while it more violently enraged interventionist reviewers, it intimidated and restrained them in some cases. At least they were more restrained than they would have been if the book were not so formidable an exhibit of arduous and exhaustive scholarship.

Dexter Perkins reviewed the book about as gingerly and cautiously in the *New York Times Book Review*, May 11, 1952, as, earlier, Bemis had handled the Sanborn volume. He was, apparently, also somewhat concerned about a possible comment on his review in future editions of my *Historical Blackout*. Aside from reiterating his well-known theme, to the effect that President Roosevelt was reluctantly pushed into war by the force of an ardent and alarmed public opinion, Perkins mainly contented himself with berating the "animus" and "bitterness" shown by Mr. Tansill. This bitterness appeared to consist, actually, in producing documentary proof that the Roosevelt-Hull diplomacy constituted one of the major public crimes of human history.

The review by Basil Rauch in the *Herald Tribune Book Review*, June 1, 1952, was as brash and reckless as was Rauch's own book, *Roosevelt from Munich to Pearl Harbor*. It was not unfairly referred to by one reader as "a masterpiece of misrepresentation." As the Byzantine emperor Basil II earned the title of "Basil the Bulgar-Slayer," so Rauch can surely be awarded the title of "Basil the Creator." As I have shown in my brochure, *Rauch on Roosevelt*, Professor Rauch, in his book, created for Mr. Roosevelt a foreign policy which bore very slight resemblance to the one which the President actually followed. So, in his review of the Tansill volume, he created a book which had little relationship to the one he was supposed to be reviewing. The book and the review must both be read to allow one to become fully aware of the extent to which this is true. Rauch accused Tansill of making statements and drawing conclusions which had no documentary support whatever, though in the book itself hundreds of footnotes and references to acres of documents were presented to buttress Tansill's statements.

Back Door to War was tardily and loftily smeared in the *Saturday Review of Literature* of August 2, 1952, by Professor Lindsay Rogers of Columbia University. Professor Rogers is not a "court historian," but he was the leading court political scientist and court jester in the original New Deal "brain trust." He pays tribute to "the enormous industry of five years which this ponderous tome required." But he tells the reader that it has been "largely wasted" because Professor Tansill has outdone the late Dr. Beard in espousing the "devil theory of history" and has interlarded his book with distressing "diatribes."

The devil theory of history appears to reside in the fact that Professor Tansill adopts a critical attitude toward the Roosevelt foreign policy and that he assigns considerable personal responsibility to President Roosevelt for the course of our foreign affairs after 1933. The "diatribes" are occasional penetrating comments on Roosevelt and his foreign policy which, had they been directed against the critics of Mr. Roosevelt, would have been praised by Professor Rogers as distilled wisdom and brilliant bons mots.

The Tansill book was belatedly reviewed at length in the *Nation*, October 4, 1952, by Professor Charles C. Griffin, who had reviewed the Beard volume in the *American Historical Review*. It is evident from the opening sentences of the review that Professor Griffin regards any comprehensive marshaling of the facts relative to Roosevelt foreign policy as a "violent attack" upon them. The gist of the review was much the same as that by Professor Rogers in the *Saturday Review of Literature*. Both reviewers are compelled to recognize the vast amount of research which went into the preparation of the Tansill book, but Professor Griffin, like Professor Rogers, holds that all this is vitiated by Professor Tansill's cogent and penetrating characterizations, which are variously described as "opprobrious and objectionable terminology," "invective," "innuendo," "insinuation," and the like. Doubtless Professor Griffin, like Professor Rogers, would have regarded this material as brilliant and praiseworthy verbiage if it had been written in praise of the Roosevelt policy. But, at least, Professor Griffin's presentation of his views on the Tansill volume constitutes a formal and ostensible review, not a brief and casual smear, and he does concede at the end of his review that the Tansill volume has value in that it corrects the fantastic mythology which prevailed during the Second World War.

The review by Arthur Kemp in the *Freeman*, May 19, 1952, was friendly and commendatory.

Professor Tansill's book was harshly reviewed in the *American Historical Review*, October 1952, by Dean Julius W. Pratt. That the latter had lined up with our "Ministry of Truth" could have been ascertained in advance of the review by comparing his early, trenchant, anti-imperialist writings, in his books and in his articles in the *American Mercury*, with his recent *America's Colonial Experiment*. The flavor of his review could readily be anticipated. However, Dean Pratt did concede that the book was the most "weightily documented" of the revisionist works on the Second World War and that "Professor Tansill has produced a book of great learning."

One statement in the review calls for corrective comment: "The fact that a scholar with Professor Tansill's well-known views on American foreign policy was allowed the free run of confidential State Department files should lay at rest the theory that there exists a favored group of 'court historians' who speak only kind words of Rooseveltian diplomacy." While Professor Tansill did examine more documents than any other revisionist historian, he had nothing like the free access to archives and diaries which was accorded to men like Professors Langer and Gleason and Dr. Herbert Feis. Dr. Beard's attacks on the State Department favoritism eased his entry, and some of his former graduate students were in charge of important sections of the documents. Even so, he was barred from many, his notes subjected to scrutiny, and some of them confiscated.

One of the most extreme smears of the book was written by a professional historian, Professor Richard W. Van Alstyne of the University of Southern California, and published in the *Pacific Historical Review*, November 1952. Van Alstyne concluded that *Back Door to War* is "a striking monument to pedantic scholarship, but it is built on a tiny mound of historical understanding." He did, however, make one sound point: that the book has a misleading title, in that it is more a study of the origins of the Second World War than specifically of Roosevelt foreign policy.

The *New Republic* did not review the book, but the editor, Michael Straight, subjected it to the lowest and most amazing smear that any revisionist book has yet received. In the issue of June 16, 1952, Straight delivered himself of the following material, suitable for presentation by the late Mr. Ripley:

> This book is part of the devious attack on American diplomacy directed by Dr. Edmund Walsh, S.J., from Georgetown University. Tansill argues that the U.S., not Germany or Japan, was the aggressor in the Second World War....

> These are the superstitions that occupied Beard in his senility
> and focused John T. Flynn's mania for hatred. It would be easily
> dismissed, were it not such useful material for demagogues in the
> 1952 campaign.

Nothing better illustrates the shift in attitude on the part of the *New Republic* since the 1920s, when it took the lead in promoting revisionism under Herbert Croly and Robert Littell, even though Mr. Straight's mother was also financing the journal at the time.

Very interesting and relevant, as bearing on Mr. Straight's charge that Professor Tansill's book was the product of a Catholic plot to smear Rooseveltian foreign policy, is the fact that the Catholic periodical *America* reflecting the interventionist wing of American Catholic opinion, published a rather bitter attack by Father William A. Lucey upon the Tansill volume in its issue of June 14, 1952.

A very amusing and instructive example of the length to which interventionists will go in quest of smears of revisionist books is provided in the case of the *Christian Register*. This periodical is edited by Melvin Arnold, a liberal Unitarian and the head of the Beacon Press which has published the books by Paul Blanchard that have so vigorously attacked Catholic political power. Yet, being an ardent interventionist and adulator of Roosevelt foreign policy, Mr. Arnold reached out eagerly for this hostile review of the Tansill book by Father Lucey in one of the leading political organs of Jesuit Catholic journalism and reprinted it in the December 1952 issue of his own magazine.

Professor Tansill's book was reviewed in the *Mississippi Valley Historical Review*, December 1952, by Professor Ruhl Bartlett. Professor Bartlett had been put on the program of the American Historical Association at Chicago in December 1950, to criticize the paper presented at that time by Professor Tansill on the background of the American entry into the Second World War. He was somewhat roughly handled by Professor Tansill in the discussion that followed. All this was well known to the editor of the *Mississippi Valley Historical Review*. Nevertheless, he chose Professor Bartlett to review Professor Tansill's book, and the result was just what could have been expected. The flavor of the review is shown by the closing lines: "The book is unredeemed by humor, art or insight. To read it and to write about it are unrewarding tasks."

Thus far, the *Journal of Modern History* has not reviewed the book.

In the criticisms of the Tansill volume by such professional historians as Professors Harrington, Pratt, and Van Alstyne, there is one slightly humorous item, namely, the charge that Tansill does not support *all* of his contentions by citations from confidential archival material. As a matter of fact, the only honest and fair criticism of Tansill's procedure is that, like so many professional diplomatic historians, he relies *too much* on archival and allied materials when other sources of information are often far more illuminating and reliable. Nevertheless, his professorial critics contend that he never *proves* an assertion unless he brings archival material to his support, even though he may cite scores of more important types and sources of evidence. One might be led to suppose that Tansill could not prove the guilt of President Roosevelt relative to Pearl Harbor unless he could produce from the archives a confession signed in the handwriting of the late President.

From what has been set forth above, it is evident that not one professional historical journal has provided readers with a fair and objective appraisal of Professor Tansill's monumental volume, *Back Door to War.*

The majority of the newspaper reviews smeared the book, though it was warmly praised not only by the *Chicago Tribune* but by some other papers like the *Indianapolis Star.* In the newspaper reviews the dominant note was Tansill's alleged bias and bitterness—in other words, his devotion to candor and integrity. Interestingly enough, the editor of the *Cleveland Plain Dealer* was apparently so displeased by the unfair reviews that he wrote an editorial (June 8, 1952) praising the Tansill volume and commending revisionism in general.

Probably the most extreme job of smearing ever turned in on a liberal who attacked the foreign policy of Roosevelt was done on John T. Flynn, whose revisionist writings were limited to two brochures on Pearl Harbor and to a few passages in his book *The Roosevelt Myth.* Flynn had long been a special favorite of the liberal journals. He was probably the leading specialist for the *New Republic* in exposing the evils of finance capitalism. His *Security Speculation* was a masterpiece in this field. His *Graft in Business* was, perhaps, the ablest indictment of the business ideals and methods of the Harding-Coolidge era. He was one of the staff who aided Pecora in his investigation of the sins of Wall Street. He was also an assistant to Senator Gerald P. Nye in the famous munitions and armament investigation. He was at one time a member of the Board of Higher Education in New York City and a lecturer at the New School for Social Research. Few men rated higher in the esteem of eastern liberals.

But when Flynn became a leading member of the America First movement and began to oppose President Roosevelt's war policy, his erstwhile liberal admirers, who had taken to warmongering, turned on him savagely. Their animus increased when Flynn revealed the fascist trends in our war policy in his book *As We Go Marching* and when he told the truth about Pearl Harbor in two trenchant brochures. Since that time he has been the victim of incessant smearing by the totalitarian liberals and the interventionist crowd. They have done their best to drive him into penury and obscurity. Only his fighting Irish spirit has enabled him to survive. Even the *Progressive*, despite its antiwar policy, joined in the smearing.

A good sample of the irresponsibility in smearing Flynn is the statement of Arthur M. Schlesinger, Jr., in the *New York Post*, to the effect that the Yalta Conference will redound to the honor of Franklin D. Roosevelt "unless a Fascist revolution installs William Henry Chamberlin and John T. Flynn as official national historians." It so happens that Flynn has, for more than a decade now, been recognized as one of our most stalwart libertarians and individualists and has even been smeared for being such by persons in Schlesinger's intellectual circle. One of the reasons for their frenzied hatred of him is his revelation of fascist trends in Roosevelt foreign policy and its political results. Chamberlin is also conspicuous for his libertarian trends and his protests against military state capitalism.

The blackout contingent was even more successful in their attacks on Upton Close. As a result of his candid radio broadcasts on our foreign policy he was driven off the air, from the lecture platform, and out of the press, and his books on the Far East were virtually barred from circulation.

Though I have personally written nothing on revisionism relative to the Second World War beyond several brief brochures seeking to expose some of the more characteristic methods of the blackout contingent, the Smearbund has gone to work on me far more vigorously than was the case following *all* my revisionist articles and books combined after the First World War. The silent treatment has been comprehensively applied to anything I have published recently, in whatever field. When my *History of Western Civilization* appeared, in 1935, it was very glowingly reviewed on the front page of the *New York Times Book Review*, of the *Herald Tribune Books*, and of the *Saturday Review of Literature*. The *American Historical Review* gave it a long and favorable review by the foremost American authority in the field. When my *Society in Transition* was published, in 1939, the *Times* accorded it the unique honor of reviewing a college textbook on the first page of its *Book Review*. But when my *Survey of Western Civilization* and *Introduction to the History of Sociology* were published in 1947, and my *Historical Sociology* in 1948, none of the above-mentioned publications, so far as could be discovered, gave any of them so much as a book note. Apparently the movement has gone so far that authors are being suppressed or given the silent treatment for fear that they might, *later on,* publish some little truth on world affairs. The author of this chapter was naturally suspect because of his writings on the First World War.

The sub rosa activities of the blackout Smearbund have gone much further. I have been smeared as both an extreme radical and an extreme reactionary and as everything undersirable between these two extremes. One historian smeared me as a "naive isolationist," though, in actuality, I was working for sane internationalism at the time of his birth. The Smearbund has not only condemned my books to the silent treatment, barred me from all leading periodicals, and sought to dissuade publishers from accepting my books on any subject, but its members have also carried on extensive subterranean intrigue, seeking to discourage the use of my textbooks in the fields of the history of civilization and sociology, where the content of my tomes does not touch even remotely on the issues of revisionism. Going beyond my writings, the blackout "Gestapo" forced the most powerful lecture manager in the United States to drop me from his list of lecturers.

The blackout boys have not rested content with smearing those who have sought to tell the truth about the causes of the Second World War. They have now advanced to the point where they are seeking to smear those who told the truth about the causes of the

First World War. At the meeting of the American Historical Association in Boston in December 1949, two papers were read by Richard W. Leopold and Selig Adler that endeavored to undermine the established revisionist writings regarding the prelude to that conflict.[35] Adler implied that revisionism, after 1918, was, in its origins, a sort of Bolshevik plot, and that revisionist writers were, conciously or unconsciously, dupes of the Bolsheviks and unrepentant Germans. Arthur M. Schlesinger, Jr., in an article in the *Partisan Review,* [36] has even gone so far as to attack those who have written in a revisionist tone on the causes of the Civil War. The next step will be to attack the revision of historical opinion relative to the causes of the American Revolution and to find that, after all, "Big Bill" Thompson was right in his views of that conflict and in his threat to throw George V into the Chicago Ship Canal. In other words, revisionism, which only means bringing history into accord with facts, now seems to be rejected by the blackout boys as a mortal sin against Clio, the Muse of their subject. This attack on revisionism, even with respect to the First World War, is now creeping into the routine college textbooks. It provides the leitmotiv of Harrison's above-mentioned book, *This Age of Global Strife.*

Not only are books concerned primarily with an honest account of the diplomacy connected with the coming of the Second World War ignored and smeared, but similar treatment is accorded to books which even indirectly reflect on the official mythology in this area. For example, A. Frank Reel's splendid and courageous book on *The Case of General Yamashita* was rather generally attacked, and outrageously so by John H. E. Fried in the *Political Science Quarterly,* September 1950. W. T. Couch, who had done splendid work as head of the University of Chicago Press, was relieved of his post in part because of criticism of his publication of this book. The best book on Japan which has been published since Pearl Harbor, *Mirror for Americans: Japan* by Helen

---

[35]Professor Leopold's paper on "The Problem of American Intervention, 1917: An Historical Retrospect," was published in *World Politics,* April, 1950, pp. 405–25. Professor Adler's paper on "The War Guilt Question and American Disillusionment, 1918–1928," was published in the *Journal of Modern History,* March, 1951, pp. 1–28. For my reply to Adler, see the *Journal of Modern History,* September 1951.

[36]October 1949.

Mears, was allowed to die quietly by its publishers after the blackout contingent began to exert pressure against it.

While the Smearbund has usually rested content with an effort to defame and impoverish those of whom it disapproves, it went even further in the case of Lawrence Dennis and sought to jail him on the charge of "sedition." Dennis, a brilliant Harvard graduate, had served in important posts in the American diplomatic service for eight years. He had been one of the first to enlist in the Plattsburg training experiment before the First World War (1915) and had served with distinction as an officer in the war. After retiring from the diplomatic service, he was employed by leading banking and brokerage firms as an expert on foreign bonds. Like John T. Flynn, he was then a favorite of left-wing American liberals and had exposed the foreign bond frauds in the *New Republic* at about the same time that Flynn was doing a comparable piece of work on the investment trusts. He incurred the wrath of liberals by bringing out a book in 1936 entitled *The Coming American Fascism.* Here he predicted that the New Deal would wind up in a system of Fascism, whatever the name given to it, and described what the system would probably be like. The interventionists were enraged by his *Weekly Foreign Letter,* which opposed our entry into the Second World War, and by his *Dynamics of War and Revolution,* the best book written in the United States on the institutional forces pushing us into war and on the probable results of such a war. The prowar forces induced Harper & Brothers to withdraw the book almost immediately after publication.

Though Dennis is, actually, an aggressive individualist, he was accused of being an ardent fascist and was railroaded into the mass sedition trial in Washington in 1944. That the trial ended in a farce was due mainly to the fact that Dennis personally outlined and conducted the defense. But, though surely one of the most talented writers and lecturers in the United States today, he has been driven into complete obscurity; not even Regnery or Devin-Adair dares to bring out a book under his name.

Global Crusading and the Historical Blackout Are Undermining Historical Integrity[37]

The revisionist position bearing on the Second World War is more

[37] The following material is essentially that prepared for delivery before the Ameri-

firmly established factually, even on the basis of the materials which revisionist scholars are permitted to examine, than the revisionism of the 1920s was by the revelations produced after 1918. But the effective presentation of revisionist contentions is frustrated, so far as any substantial influence is concerned, over any predictable future.

Certain revisionist scholars, led by the late Charles Austin Beard, have justly protested the fact that they are not permitted anything like the same access to the relevant documents as is the case with the so-called "court historians."

This is true and deplorable, but it is not a consideration of major importance with respect to revisionism today. Revisionists already have plenty of facts. It may be safely assumed that any further revelations will only more firmly establish the revisionist position. Otherwise, all the archives and other still-secret materials would, long since, have been made available to reputable scholars, so that President Roosevelt and his administration might be cleared of unfair and inaccurate charges, founded upon limited and unreliable information. If there were nothing to hide, then, there would, obviously, be no reason for denying access to the documents. In short, the revisionist position is not likely to be shattered by any future documentary revelations. There is every prospect that it will be notably strengthened thereby, and this assumption is confirmed by some recently edited documents on the Far Eastern situation in 1937. These show that China and Japan were growing tired of friction and conflict and were about to agree that they should get together and oppose the Communists as the chief common enemy. But the American authorities looked askance at this. Instead, they encouraged and made possible the resumption of war between China and Japan.

The development of revisionism in connection with the Second World War is placed in jeopardy mainly by the hostile attitude which exists on the part of both the general public and the historical profession toward accepting the facts and their implications

---

can Historical Association in Chicago on December 29, 1950. Between the invitation to prepare the paper and the printing of the program, the writer was switched, without his knowledge, to the role of discussing papers read by others. Hence, the original address could not be given. Certain minor changes have been made better to adapt the material for inclusion in this book.

with respect to world events and American policies during the last fifteen years.

The attitude and emotions of the public during wartime have been maintained without notable change by means of persistent propaganda. There has been no such disillusionment and reversal of attitude since 1945 as took place rather rapidly after 1918. The United States seems all too likely to undertake a third bloody crusade before it is fully aware of the real causes and disastrous results of the second.

The factual justification for a reversal of public attitudes and emotions is far more extensive and impressive than was the case following the First World War. But the party which was in power during the war continued to hold office until 1953, and the potency and scope of propaganda have so increased that the emotions and convictions of wartime have been perpetuated for more than a decade after Pearl Harbor. Incidentally, this is ominous evidence of our susceptibility to propaganda as we approach the "Nineteen Eighty-Four" way of life.

The historical profession is, perhaps, even less tolerant of revisionism than is the general public. Most of those who had been leading revisionists during the 1920s espoused our second crusade, even before it exploded into war at the time of Pearl Harbor. Great numbers of historians entered into war propaganda work of one kind or another after Pearl Harbor and thus have a vested interest in perpetuating the myth of the nobility of the cause which enlisted their services. Therefore, the historical profession is oriented and powerfully fortified against any acceptance of revisionist scholarship. A number of the leading revisionists of the 1920s have now become court historians, and most of the other erstwhile revisionists refuse to admit that we were as thoroughly misled by the second crusade as by the first.

As a result of all this and numerous other factors and forces hostile to revisionism, the situation is not encouraging to any historians who might otherwise be inclined to undertake honest research in the field. To do so would mean departmental antagonism, loss of promotion, and possibly discharge from their posts. Those not dissuaded by such considerations have to face irresponsible smearing. The very idea or concept of revisionism is now anathema and is actually under fire at the hands of a number of prominent historians.

In case a few historians are not discouraged or intimidated by professional hostility or the prospect of irresponsible smearing, and remain determined to do substantial work on the actual causes and merits of the Second World War, there is every likelihood that their efforts will prove futile so far as publication is concerned. Forthright revisionist material, however scholarly, is, for all practical purposes, excluded from publication in the great majority of our newspapers and periodicals. Only two small publishing houses in the United States have been willing to publish books embodying revisionist facts and conclusions, and they often require subsidies beyond the resources of the average private scholar. Few historians are going to be lured by the prospect of devoting years of research to a project and then be compelled to store away their completed manuscripts in a filing cabinet. They are more likely to be "practical" and fall in line with the court historians, which is the path to professional prestige and prosperity today.

When any scholar defies professional hostility and successfully gambles upon the slight prospect of publication for the results of his labors, there is little likelihood that his book will have anything like the same influence on the modification of public opinion as did the outstanding revisionist volumes of the 1920s and early 1930s. The probability is that any substantial and meritorious revisionist volume will be given the silent treatment—that is, it will not be reviewed at all in the majority of newspapers and periodicals.

When a newspaper or a periodical decides actually to review a revisionist book, it has available, as we have noted, a large corps of hatchet men, both on its own staff and drawn from eager academicians, who can be relied upon to attack and smear revisionist volumes and to eulogize the works of court historians who seek to perpetuate the traditional mythology.

There is, thus, very little probability that even the most substantial and voluminous revisionist writing on the Second World War can have any decisive impact upon public opinion for years to come. One only needs to contrast the enthusiastic reception accorded to Walter Millis's *Road to War* in 1935 with the general ignoring or smearing of the much more substantial and meritorious volume by William Henry Chamberlin, *America's Second Crusade,* in 1950.

The probability is that revisionism, in relation to the Second World War, will never be widely accepted directly on the basis of its factual merit. It will only become palatable, if ever, after we have suffered some devastating economic or political disaster which causes the American public to reverse its attitudes and policies on world affairs and to seek an ideological justification through espousing revisionist contentions. But it is obvious that it will probably require a tremendous shock—a veritable military and political catastrophe—to bring about the degree of disillusionment and realism required to produce any such result.

There is infinitely greater cause for a reversal of public attitudes today than there was in 1923, when Woodrow Wilson remarked to James Kerney: "I should like to see Germany clean up France, and I should like to see Jusserand [the French ambassador] and tell him so to his face."[38] But, as indicated above, this ample factual basis for a comparable revision of public opinion has produced no substantial public or historical disillusionment with respect to our second crusade. Disillusionment has not even gone far enough to produce tolerance toward those who seek to explain realistically the historical basis of the transformation of Stalin from the "noble ally" of a decade ago into the current incarnation of Satan himself.

As is implied above, even though the tenets of revisionism, with respect to the Second World War, may at some distant time achieve popular acceptance in the wake of overwhelming national disaster, this will not necessarily mean any reinstatement of objective historical scholarship. The probability is that any such future period may also be one in which we will have completed the transition into "Nineteen Eighty-Four" society, which will crush out all semblance of historical freedom and objectivity. As we shall point out in a moment, ominous trends in this direction have already set in.

What we may conclude from all this is that both the public and the historians seem quite likely to be effectively protected against any immediate ravages at the hands of revisionism. But what they will pay for this "protection" may be the greatest disaster which historical science has ever encountered since the era of the cave paintings of the Stone Age.

[38] James Kerney, *The Political Education of Woodrow Wilson* (New York: The Century Company, 1926), p. 476.

However much we may recoil from the prospect, there seems a strong probability that we are now entering the twilight of historical science. This is the penalty which has been exacted, so far as history and historians are concerned, for ballyhooing and defending crusades rather than seeking the truth. History has been an intellectual casualty in both world wars, and there is much doubt that it can be rehabilitated during the second half of the century. Indeed, there is every prospect that it will become more and more an instrument and adjunct of official propaganda—a supine instrument of our "Ministry of Truth."

Many will counter these assertions by contending that the elaborate development of the methodology of historical research and exposition in our day is an adequate safeguard against the eclipse of historical integrity, prestige, and independence. But technical methodology is of little significance if those who utilize it are dominated by intense emotions or personal ambition rather than by a desire to ascertain the facts. Ample footnotes are no guarantee of accuracy or objectivity. They may only document falsehood. Formal compliance with technical methodology may only enable an historian to distort or falsify material in more complicated and ostensibly impressive fashion. If one does not wish to ascertain or state the facts, then the most effective methods of locating, classifying, and expounding the facts are nullified and of no avail.[39]

Only a generation or so ago it was believed by most thoughtful historians that nationalism and militarism were the chief obstacle and menace to historical objectivity. It was assumed that an international outlook would make for truth and tolerance. It was held that, if we understood the extensive and complicated international contributions to all national cultures, most forms of hatred and bias would disappear. Internationalists then stressed the blessings of peace. The great majority of them were pacifists, admired peace, meant peace when they said peace, and repudiated all thought of military crusades for peace.

Had internationalism retained the same traits that it possessed even as late as the mid-1930s, these assumptions as to the beneficent impact of internationalism upon historical writing might

---

[39]See my extended discussion, *The Court Historians versus Revisionism,* privately printed, 1952.

have been borne out in fact. But, during the years since 1937, the older pacific internationalism has been virtually extinguished, and internationalism has itself been conquered by militarism and aggressive globaloney.

Militarism was, formerly, closely linked to national arrogance. Today it stalks behind the semantic disguise of internationalism, which has become a cloak for national aggrandizement and imperialism. Programs of world domination by great powers that would have left Napoleon, or even Hitler, aghast are now presented with a straight face as international crusades for freedom, peace, sweetness, and light. Peace is to be promoted and ultimately realized through bigger and more frequent wars. The obvious slogan of the internationalists of our day, who dominate the historical profession as well as the political scene, is "perpetual war for perpetual peace." This, it may be noted, is also the ideological core of "Nineteen Eighty-Four" society.

Borne along by an irresistible tide of crusading fervor for over a decade and a half, most historians have fallen in line with this ominous revolution in the nature, influence, and goals of internationalism. Among well-known historians, this transition is probably most perfectly exemplified by the ideological shift in the thinking and writings of Carlton J. H. Hayes, once an able and eloquent critic of militarism, imperialism, and international meddling. The majority of our historians now support international crusades—the "savior with the sword" complex—with far more vehemence, obsession, and intolerance than were exhibited by the most ardent nationalistic historians of the past. In my opinion, Droysen, Treitschke, Lamartine, Michelet, Macaulay, and Bancroft were calm scholars and pacific publicists compared to our present-day historical inciters to global crusades such as James Thomson Shotwell, Edward Mead Earle, Thomas A. Bailey, Samuel Flagg Bemis, Henry Steele Commager, Allan Nevins, Arthur M. Schlesinger, Jr., and the like. To resist the savior-with-the-sword program today is akin to treason politically, and professionally suicidal for any historian. He is immediately smeared as an "isolationist," which is today a far worse crime before the bar of historical judgment than overt forgery of documents.

Some historians admit that this crusading by the nationalistic and militaristic wolf in the sheep's clothing of internationalism and its global wars for peace may eliminate objectivity from the history of recent events. But they contend that historical serenity may, nevertheless, survive when treating more remote eras and personalities. This is unlikely, because the emotions that have nullified historical objectivity in dealing with the history of the last twenty years are projected back into our portrayal and interpretations of the more distant past.

Germans from Arminius onward are now interesting chiefly as precursors of Hitler in one way or another. Since Hitler was a neurotic, and perhaps a paranoid, all German history is portrayed as a product of paranoia, and the only real solution is the elimination of all Germans.[40] Paul Winkler has written about a "thousand-year conspiracy" of the Germans to incite wars against civilization,[41] and Lord Robert Vansittart would, according to his *Lessons of My Life,*[42] extend the period of plotting to nearly two thousand years. William M. McGovern, in his book *From Luther to Hitler,*[43] has already implied that everything in German history since Luther is mainly significant as preparing the way for Hitler. Bishop Bossuet, actually the great ideological apologist for paternalistic absolutism, becomes the first French fascist because his doctrines were the chief political inspiration of Marshal Pétain. Proudhon, about whom historians long wrangled as to whether he is to be most accurately classified as an anarchist or as a socialist, is now revealed by J. Salwyn Schapiro to be a father of French fascism. At present it seems impossible to write a biography of Ivan the Terrible without indicating the deep similarity between Ivan and Stalin, and devoting as much attention to the latter as to the former. The menace of Genghis Khan and Tamerlane has become historically important mainly as a warning against the current challenge of the Kremlin. Serious scholars have even sought to interpret Socrates, long supposed to have been the first martyr to the freedom of thought and expression, as the father of fascism.[44] Plato, of late, has frequently been described as the

[40]See Richard Brickner, *Is Germany Incurable?* (Philadelphia: J.B. Lippincott Company, 1943).

[41]*The Thousand-Year Conspiracy; Secret Germany Behind the Mask* (New York: Charles Scribner's Sons, 1943).

[42]New York: Alfred A. Knopf, 1943. See my review of Vansittart in *The Progressive,* September 17, 1945.

[43]Boston: Houghton Mifflin Company, 1941.

[44]A. D. Winspear and Tom Silverberg, *Who Was Socrates?* (New York: Cordon Company, Inc., 1939).

outstanding Greek fascist. Even the great warriors of mid-Eastern antiquity are portrayed as prototypes of Hitler and Stalin. The conquering heroes of the Sung, Tang, Ming, and Manchu dynasties of China only prepared the way for Mao Tse-tung. Indeed, Richard Match, in the *New York Times,* December 30, 1951, suggested that the vicissitudes of Jade Star, the favorite concubine of Kublai Khan, hold many lessons "for troubled China today."

Some concede the current dangers to historical science which lie in the factors briefly described above. But they gain solace and reassurance from the assumption that the strong emotions which have gripped historical science for several decades will soon subside and that the objectivity and tolerance that preceded the First World War will ultimately reassert themselves.

Unfortunately, all the main political, social, and cultural trends of our time point ominously in the opposite direction. The discovery of politicians that the "giddy-minds-and-foreign-quarrels" strategy is the most certain key to political success and extended tenure of office is rapidly forcing the world into the pattern of "Nineteen Eighty-Four" society, if, indeed, this has not already been achieved. Historical writing and interpretation are rapidly being brought into line with the needs and mental attitudes of such a political regime.

The rhetorical basis of the global crusades of our day—"perpetual war for perpetual peace"—is the most gigantic and ominous example in all history of the "Newspeak" and "doublethink" of "Nineteen Eighty-Four" semantics. We have already pointed out that it is also the cornerstone of "Nineteen Eighty-Four" ideology. The security measures alleged to be necessary to promote and execute global crusades are rapidly bringing about the police state in hitherto free nations, including our own. Any amount of arbitrary control over political and economic life, the most extensive invasions of civil liberties, the most extreme witch-hunting, and the most lavish expenditures, can all be demanded and justified on the basis of alleged "defense" requirements, without even examining the validity of the need for such defensive measures. This is precisely the psychological attitude and procedural policy which dominates "Nineteen Eighty-Four" society.

The emotional tensions essential to the support of perpetual global crusading have facilitated the dominion of propaganda over almost every phase of intellectual and public life. The books by James Burnham, *The Managerial Revolution, The Machiavellians, The Struggle for the World, The Coming Defeat of Communism,* and *Containment or Liberation?* have helped to prepare us ideologically for the reception of "Nineteen Eighty-Four" institutions, political techniques, and mental attitudes. They "soften us up" for the more willing reception of a system of military managerialism.

The hysterical reaction following Orson Welles's bogus radio broadcast on October 30, 1938, depicting an invasion from Mars, emphasizes the American capacity for credulity and shows how wartime propaganda in the next war, whether cold, hot, or phony, can readily duplicate anything of the kind portrayed in *Nineteen Eighty-Four.* Those who are skeptical on this point will do well to read Hadley Cantril's book *The Invasion from Mars.*[45]

The fact that our propaganda agencies have been able to hold public opinion fairly well within the confines of the illusions of wartime for over eight years is sufficient evidence that our propaganda machinery is equal to all the emergencies and responsibilities likely to be imposed upon it by "Nineteen Eighty-four" conditions. From five to seven years is as long as Oceania can maintain fever hatred of either Eurasia or Eastasia in *Nineteen Eighty-Four.*

We have already richly developed the "Newspeak" and the "doublethink" semantics of *Nineteen Eighty-Four* where the War Department is known as the "Ministry of Peace," the propaganda and public lying are conducted by the "Ministry of Truth," the espionage system and torture chambers are administered by the "Ministry of Love," and the department which is entrusted with the problem of keeping the masses subdued by attributing their drab life and grinding poverty to the need for defense is known as the "Ministry of Plenty."[46]

Thomas A. Bailey approvingly warns us that, unless we wish to have greater deception of the public by the executive department of the federal government, we must free the executive of hampering congressional control in foreign affairs: "Deception of the

---

[45]Hadley Cantril, Hazel Gaudet, and Herta Hertzog, *The Invasion from Mars; a Study in the Psychology of Panic; with the Complete Script of the Orson Welles Broadcast* (Princeton, N.J.: Princeton University Press, 1940).

[46]See Orwell, *op. cit., passim.*

people may, in fact, become increasingly necessary, unless we are willing to give our leaders in Washington a freer hand."[47] We appear likely to get both greater deception and more executive irresponsibility.

These ominous trends have their clear implications for the future of historical science. In *Nineteen Eighty-Four,* Orwell portrays it as necessary to intimidate and hire servile bureaucrats to falsify current history. This may not be necessary for a time, as we ourselves enter the "Nineteen Eighty-Four" way of life. Indeed, the writings and intrigues of our interventionist and war-minded historians have been a powerful force propelling us in this direction. In the opinion of the writer, James Thomson Shotwell, who has been the most influential of our interventionist historians for more than a third of a century, has done more than any other American intellectual figure to speed us on our way into the "Nineteen Eighty-Four" pattern of public life. Edward Mead Earle, Henry Steele Commager, Allan Nevins, Arthur M. Schlesinger, Jr., and a host of younger men are now following enthusiastically in his footsteps.

Among other things, Shotwell was one of the chief inventors of the myth and fantasy of an "aggressive nation" and "aggressive war," which have become a basic semantic fiction and instrument of "Nineteen Eighty-Four" international jargon, policy, and procedure. It has been adopted enthusiastically by Oceania, Eurasia, and Eastasia. This phraseology has now lost all semblance of ethics, realism, logic, and consistency, however effective it may be in international propaganda. Indeed, as Henry W. Lawrence pointed out nearly twenty years ago, the concept of "aggressive war" never possessed any historical realism:

> The harmonizing of national policies must deal with fundamentals; with the things that commonly have caused wars. The moral right to keep on possessing the best regions of the earth is directly balanced by the right to fight and capture them. It is amazing that so few people will admit this axiom of international morality. Popular opinion is widely befogged in the more comfortable countries by the childish notion that an aggressive war is wicked but a defensive war is righteous. They are, of course, precisely equal in moral quality, so long as war is the only adequate instrument by which vested wrongs can be righted and national needs supplied.

[47]*The Man in the Street: The Impact of American Public Opinion on Foreign Policy* (New York: The Macmillan Company, 1948), p. 13.

> The next rational step toward a tolerable world peace would be the broadcasting of this truth throughout Great Britain, France, and the United States. It is already familiar to the peoples of Germany, Italy, and Japan.[48]

Since 1929, and especially since 1937, the "aggressor myth" has been made the basis of the unrealistic and hypocritical international ethics and jurisprudence associated invariably with "Nineteen Eighty-Four" semantics and propaganda in which the enemy is always an aggressor and wars are fought to stop aggression. Since the Second World War the "aggressor" has become the nation or coalition that is defeated in war, whatever the responsibility for starting hostilities. Being defeated, it must be punished and its leaders exterminated. Driven home by the Nuremberg and Tokyo trials, this subterfuge has given advance notice to leaders in any future wars that they must not take the risk of being defeated, no matter what horrors they have to unleash to assure victory. In this way the internationalists who falsely pose as protagonists of peace have not only produced a condition of more or less permanent war but have also made it certain that future wars will become ever more savage and devastating. No possible means of destruction can be spared to assure victory.[49]

The majority of the writings of our historians on recent world history during the last decade and a half could be warmly accepted by an American "Ministry of Truth." The presidential address of Admiral Samuel Eliot Morison, given before the American Historical Association at Chicago on December 29, 1950, with its eulogy of war and the myth-mongers, could easily have been an official assignment executed for such a ministry. He even preferred to provide a picture of himself in a naval uniform to be used for the program rather than to have himself portrayed in the lowly and pacific garb of a scholar. One of the most eminent of our diplomatic historians has actually proclaimed that the most commendable result of the Second World War was that it provided us with a new and stronger opponent after Hitler had been overthrown. Even our court historians work without compulsion. Few historians have been critical of the trend toward the "Nineteen Eighty-Four" patterns, and probably many of them, suffering

[48]"Peace Costs Too Much," *Christian Century,* October 10, 1934, p. 1279.
[49]F. J. P. Veale, *Advance to Barbarism* (Appleton, Wis.: C.C. Nelson Publishing Company, 1953).

from autointoxication with globaloney, have not even recognized the trend. Some who do recognize it are so obsessed that they eulogize it. Such is the case with Henry Steele Commager in his article, "The Lessons of April 6, 1917," appearing in the *New York Times Magazine* of April 6, 1952; and with Waldo G. Leland, who proudly details the services of American historians in our "Ministry of Truth" from the First World War to the present time in an article on "The Historians and the Public in the United States" in the *Revista de Historia de America,* June 1952. Those who have sought to spread the alarm have been slapped down and smeared.

The impact of "Nineteen Eighty-Four" pressures on our historical writing now appears to have become more rapid and impressive than was apparent in the years immediately following the war. The newspapers on January 14, 1951, announced that President Truman was establishing a corps of court historians to prepare an acceptable official history of world events and American policy.[50] The avowed purpose was to protect American citizens from the lies to be found in historical works written by "Communist imperialist historians." It was implied that Admiral Morison would have general direction of the group. They would operate in conjunction with the official historians already at work within the armed services and the State Department. It may fairly be assumed that any historians who differ with the official texts and interpretations will be regarded as agents of "Communist imperialism," whatever their prior record of hostility to the communist way of life. It is only a step from this to the rewriting of the newspapers, which was the task of Winston Smith, the central figure in Orwell's *Nineteen Eighty-Four.*[51]

[50]This action was forecast in a letter from President Truman to Admiral Morison on December 22, 1950, read by the Admiral before he delivered his presidential address before the American Historical Association in Chicago on December 29. See *American Historical Review,* April, 1951, pp. 711–12. For a summary of the work of American historians under the aegis of our "Ministry of Truth," see W. G. Leland, "The Historians and the Public in the United States," in *Revista de Historia de America,* June 1952, pp. 64 ff.

[51]In *Time,* March 26, 1951, p. 19, it is pointed out that President Truman is very sensitive about his future "niche in history." If he is able to appoint the historians who will write the official history of his times and smear those who seek to tell the truth, he should fare very well. Indeed, Mr. Truman may not need paid official historians to prepare his apotheosis. Henry Steele Commager has already rushed to his aid in this respect and has predicted that history will vindicate the soundness of Mr. Truman's major policies, especially those connected with globaloney, the

There is, of course, an element of sardonic humor in all this. Actually, the "Communist imperialist historians" of Soviet Russia are almost fanatical partisans of the Roosevelt foreign policy which brought us into the Second World War to aid Russia. Hence, if any American historians might be suspected of "Communist imperialist" attitudes and tendencies, it is the interventionist group who operate the blackout and oppose revisionism.

Though this program and trend constitute probably the greatest threat to freedom and objectivity in historical writing in modern times, there has been no evidence of any alarm or protest on the part of the leading American historians. Indeed, on January 29, 1951, the *New York Herald Tribune* announced that some 875 historians and other social scientists had joined in a public statement warmly endorsing the cold war and Secretary Acheson's policy: "We support the present policy and insist that it be continued and developed without flinching. Actually, it is neither more nor less than the world-wide application of the principles of the Declaration of Independence, the Gettysburg Address, and the other basic policy declarations." This statement not only points up the apathy of historians to the threat to their professional independence but also emphasizes their levity in regard to historical accuracy. The authors of the Declaration of Independence and of the Gettysburg Address were both inveterate opponents of our being involved in "foreign entanglements."

The statement also serves potently to illustrate the transformation of the mental attitude of the members of the American Historical Association who listened with respect and warm approval, in 1916, to the noble address of its president, George Lincoln Burr, on "The Freedom of History." Indeed, there is a well-founded rumor that the idea of creating an official corps of court historians did not originate with President Truman but was passed on to him by influential antirevisionist historians who envisaged the program as an effective way to check and intimidate revisionist scholars. That some English historians are aware of the danger is evident from the recent book of Herbert Butterfield, *History*

---

cold war, and our preparation for a "Nineteen Eighty-Four" social order. Even this, however, has not satisfied Mr. Truman's urge for the affectionate caresses of Clio. He "jumped the gun" in the spring of 1952 by coauthoring his own history of himself and his public deeds, *Mr. President* (New York: Farrar, Straus and Young).

and Human Relations, in which he criticizes the "independent" historians who are hired by the Foreign Office and other governmental departments but claim to set forth the record with complete detachment.

It is quite apparent that what our officialdom fears are not the lies of "Communist imperialist historians," which could scarcely reach, much less influence, the mass of American citizens, but the truth that might be told by native American historians of long lineage, the highest patriotic motives, and complete loyalty to the American way of life as it existed before 1937. Incidentally, this trend also means that, whereas revisionism after the Second World War is difficult and frustrated, it may be nonexistent and outlawed after the third world war.

That the new policy started bearing fruit immediately was amply demonstrated at the meeting of the American Historical Association in New York City in December 1951. The official historians were present in large numbers and some fourteen of them were on the program. The Army historians were the most conspicuous, with eleven men on the program as compared with two for the State Department and one for the Navy. This was in addition to the quasi-official court historians and the blackout contingent among the civilian historians, who dominated most of the programs devoted to diplomatic history.

Not only is there to be an official history of the United States and its foreign policy, conceived in terms of the wisdom and necessity of current "Nineteen Eighty-Four" trends, but there is also planned a history of all mankind along similar lines for "Oceania" (the United States, the Atlantic Pact nations, and Latin America). The United Nations Educational, Scientific, and Cultural Organization (UNESCO) has recently announced the plan to prepare a six-volume history of mankind at a cost of $400,000, to be directed by Julian Huxley and edited by Ralph E. Turner. There can be no doubt from the prospectus that the gigantic work will have an international slant. Such an historical treatise might well be a great contribution to human knowledge and international understanding. But the auspices and sources of support will create great difficulties for Huxley, Turner, and their associates in preventing the book from falling into a frame of reference designed to show that mankind has been moving ahead from the days of *Pithecanthropus erectus* in order to evolve the form of the world policy which is hastening us into the "Nineteen Eighty-Four" system of life.

Occasionally, if very rarely, the ghost of Charles Austin Beard comes forth to stalk through the historical council chambers and to rebuke historians for their voluntary servitude in the "Ministry of Truth." A notable example was the paper read by Professor Howard K. Beale before the American Historical Association in Washington on December 28, 1952, on "The Professional Historian: His Theory and His Practice."

It is obvious that our historians, even those today most congenial to the global crusading which is leading us into the "Nineteen Eighty-Four" setup, may well take warning. If the transition is followed by severe disillusionment and a reversal of existing public attitudes, the now popular trends in historical writing may be sharply curtailed or even become the vestibule to torture chambers.

Even though current trends in our world policy continue during the early stages of our entry into the "Nineteen Eighty-Four" regime, our historians who now warmly embrace militarism, the crusading spirit, and war hysteria, may be overconfident. In a harsh, totalitarian society, even slight ideological deviations become heresies punishable by liquidation. General sympathy with the system does not assure safety. One has only to recall Hitler's purge of June and July, 1934, and Stalin's purges of Trotskyites and his later purges even of Stalinites who did not become sufficiently aware in time of the latest interpretations of Soviet philosophy and strategy.

Henry Steele Commager, one of our most ardent interventionist historians, and, hence, one of the profession most responsible for the current intellectual atmosphere of this country, has recently protested against the growing intellectual intolerance and witch-hunting, especially in the field of education. Commager may well be reminded that such a protest may furnish the basis for his liquidation. In a totalitarian society one cannot pick and choose which elements of totalitarianism he will accept and which he will reject. All phases must be accepted with enthusiasm and without protest.[52]

[52]Interestingly enough, Commager is a renegade revisionist. One should consult his veritable "rave" review of Charles C. Tansill's *America Goes to War* in the *Yale Review,* June 1938, pp. 855-57.

Another important fact to remember is that the mature "Nineteen Eighty-Four" society is highly hostile to the very conception of history. The public must be cut off from the past so that there will be no feeling of nostalgia for the happier times of previous eras. Our first stage of "Nineteen Eighty-Four" experience may only extinguish honest historical writing, but the fully developed "Nineteen Eighty-Four" regime will obliterate history entirely.

Many will doubtless regard the prediction of any imminence of our entry into "Nineteen Eighty-Four" patterns as completely fantastic, somewhat akin to astrological forecasts. The fact is, however, that, in many basic essentials, we have already arrived. With a third world war we shall be there completely and inescapably. Even the fear of a third world war may suffice. As Lewis Mumford well warned us in *Air Affairs,* March 1947, the fear of atomic warfare may suffice to impose on us a military regime more obstructive to freedom of thought and action than either world war was able to create. By 1953 we seemed to have arrived, earlier than anticipated by most, at the precise condition that Mumford predicted. The only way of averting such a calamity both to all human decencies and to the very existence of historical science, is to reveal the facts before the chains are fastened on us and the lock is closed.

This is only another way of stating that a robust revisionism is our only hope of deliverance, if there be one, at this late date. For this reason one may safely maintain that revisionism is not only the major issue in the field of historical writing today but also the supreme moral and intellectual concern of our era. Those who oppose it, whether historians or others, are only hastening and assuring their own destruction.

But I believe that few revisionists could be so devoid of decent sentiments that they would welcome vindication at the hands of the ruthless bureaucrats of a "Nineteen Eighty-Four" regime. Most of them would prefer timely repentance on the part of the blackout boys and the global crusaders rather than a form of vindication which would seal their own doom as well as that of their current opponents.

Note: An English View of the
Historical Blackout

The editor sent copies of his brochures on *The Struggle Against the Historical Blackout, The Court Historians versus Revisionism,* and *Rauch on Roosevelt* to one of the most distinguished of English publicists, authors, and military historians, who wrote me the following letter relative to the historical blackout in general and in England in particular. Being aware of the retaliation which might be meted out to him in the American scholarly and book world, I am withholding his name, but it is one that is internationally known and respected:

> Thank you for your very kind letter and the pamphlets, which I have read with enthusiastic interest. I love your phrases: "The Court Historians" and "the Blackout Boys." How delightfully descriptive! But what a revelation these last seven years have been of the strength and power of both these classes of people and their myriad supporters in the Press and among the people.
>
> To you and me, who lived in the mentally-free world of pre-1914, the determined rush of the historical Gadarenes into the sea of falsehood and distortion has been an astounding phenomenon. Which of us would have believed, in that first decade of the century, that the values which then seemed so firmly established in the historical profession could disappear so easily and rapidly, leaving only a tiny company of unheeded and derided protestors to lament their loss? And I must admit that the protestors in the U.S.A. are more numerous and courageous than they are in this blessed land of freedom which used to make such a fuss about its Magna Carta, the execution of Charles I, and other so-called landmarks in dealing with tyranny.
>
> Here we are, a nation of fifty million. Our *official* historian has just published his first book on the Norwegian campaign which shows, with official authority, that we were planning exactly the same aggression against Norway as the Germans, for which later the wretched Admiral Raeder was given a life sentence. But not one voice has been raised in England to say that, now that it is known that we were just as bad as he was, he might be let out. And I know that, if I wrote to the *Times,* it would not go in. I will not deny that there are a few Beards, Chamberlins, Tansills, and Barnes' over here. But they do not find publishers here as they do with you, for which I give yours full marks. In this blessed sceptical isle and ancient land of the free, Revisionism is gagged. You must keep yours going at all costs or the darkness descends.

My correspondent's impressions need correction in one respect: apparently he imagines that American publishers are more hospitable toward revisionist books than the English. He does not realize that, aside from Dr. Beard's books, all the revisionist volumes thus far published in the United States have been brought out by two small publishers. No large commercial publisher has brought out a revisionist volume since Pearl Harbor.

How "Nineteen Eighty-Four" Trends Threaten American Peace, Freedom, and Prosperity

We know too that vast armaments are arising on every side and that the work of creating them employs men and women by the millions. It is natural, however, for us to conclude that such employment is false employment, that it builds no permanent structures and creates no consumers' goods for the maintenance of a lasting prosperity. We know that nations guilty of these follies inevitably face the day when either their weapons of destruction must be used against their neighbors or when an unsound economy like a house of cards will fall apart.
— FRANKLIN DELANO ROOSEVELT, speech at Buenos Aires, December 1, 1936

Winston sat back against the window sill. It was no use going on. . . . Within twenty years at the most, he reflected, the huge and simple question, "Was life better before the Revolution than it is now?" would have ceased once and for all to be answerable. . . . And when memory failed and written records were falsified— when that happened, the claim of the Party to have improved the conditions of human life had got to be accepted, because there did not exist, and never again could exist, any standard against which it could be tested.
— GEORGE ORWELL, *Nineteen Eighty-Four*, pp. 92–93

American Prosperity, Foreign Policy, and Domestic Political Strategy

In 1917, and again in 1941, the government of the United States decided that it was in the national interest to participate in world wars. In both instances, economic arguments, among others, were advanced in support of that point of view. American entry into both world wars has since been related by historians, at least in part, to economic factors. During the late 1930s, economic conditions were particularly favorable to the launching of an armament and war economy. In 1938, despite the New Deal measures which provided indispensable relief to the poverty-stricken, there were still about ten million persons unemployed. Relief payments, in total, were higher than in 1933 and 1934. Only the armament program and the war economy which were established after 1939 brought temporary prosperity.

Today, gigantic armaments and the maintenance of a war economy are once more ascribed to national interest. The high level of production and employment since 1945 has been based mainly on consumer demands which could not be met during the war, on postwar foreign relief, on the armament program, and on the war preparations which started in 1947. The latter program, even before the Korean episode, was costing the United States, directly and indirectly, about $25 billion a year. It will about quadruple this sum in 1952 and 1953. By the summer of 1952, about $150 billion will have been allocated for armament expenditures in the immediate future. Every prospect points toward spending vastly more rather than less on arms for years to come and toward the continuation of economic and military aid to Europe beyond the date originally envisaged in the Marshall Plan and on a larger scale. At the Lisbon conference in February 1952, it was announced that some $300 billion would be spent on European defense between then and the end of 1954. In the light of the financial status of the European NATO countries, it is obvious that if this sum is actually raised and used, the bulk will come from the United States. If the cold war eventually develops into a hot war, its results are bound to be devastating to our economic life, even though we are lucky enough (which is very unlikely) to escape wholesale bombing of our cities, factories, and railroads.

In the light of these facts, it is obvious that the whole question of lasting prosperity for the mass of our countrymen is inseparably connected with our foreign policy, international relations, political strategy, and war psychology. The future of our economy is today far more dependent upon the policies of politicians and military leaders than upon the work of inventors or the activities of bankers and businessmen. Our technology is already capable of producing ever-increasing abundance. The depression following 1929 and subsequent developments have chastened financiers and businessmen and subjected their operations to more effective supervision and control. Therefore, if they were able to operate our technology on the basis of sound business sense, it is likely that we could enjoy relative and prolonged prosperity, even under what remains of our capitalistic system.

But today partisan political strategy overrides business independence and sagacity, and the manner in which we shall utilize our technology is keyed more to vote-getting and the associated military program than to producing goods and services and assuring human well-being. Prior to the depression, following 1929, our increasingly efficient technology was hampered and distorted by the financial manipulations of the great investment bankers and other masters of finance capitalism. Today, it is even more dangerously at the mercy of politicians who desire to guide and control our economic efforts in such a manner as will assure them victory in election campaigns, extend their tenure of office, and postpone embarrassing depressions. They are aided and abetted by military leaders who discern the opportunity to put the Pentagon group in a position of greater prestige and power than was ever enjoyed by the Prussian military caste in Imperial Germany. Support is also given by the organized peace movement now dedicated to perpetual peace through perpetual war against "aggressors," by starry-eyed internationalists, and by oil magnates who believe that they require an internationalist policy to protect their far-flung interests and possessions. John Foster Dulles is the leading spokesman for the latter group.

For about a decade and a half, the dominant political strategy has revolved mainly around using war psychology of one type or another to insure political advantage and continued tenure of office. There is little prospect of achieving a prosperous peacetime economy of any permanence unless we can check this exploitation of war psychology by short-sighted politicians and unless we are able to create lasting prosperity, mainly on the basis of an ever more efficient home economy, combined with all the rational foreign relations and external trade which our age requires and permits.

George Orwell May Replace Edward Bellamy as the Prophet of Our Future

In 1888 Edward Bellamy published an immensely popular and influential book entitled *Looking Backward*. The main thesis of this book was that the ever-growing efficiency of machinery would ultimately assure for mankind increased income, greater prosperity and security, more leisure, better educational opportunities, and more freedom. Bellamy's optimistic picture of the future was shared for more than half a century by most literate Americans, whether or not they had ever actually read the book.

A little over sixty years after Bellamy's book appeared, the brilliant English novelist and publicist, George Orwell, brought out in 1949 another profound book of prophecy entitled *Nineteen Eighty-Four*. This book, based upon a keen analysis of trends in the preceding quarter of a century, sharply challenged the optimistic spirit and social prophecies of Bellamy's utopia. Orwell predicted that, instead of universal prosperity, peace, and freedom for the masses, perpetual war, mainly phony, accompanied by permanent austerity and a rigorous regimentation of life, thought, and action, will be the pattern of human behavior during an indefinite period of the future.

Though it is written mainly in the form of a novel, Orwell's book is the keenest and most penetrating work produced in this generation on the current trends in national policy and world affairs. To discuss world trends today without reference to the Orwell frame of reference is not unlike writing on biology without reference to Darwin, Mendel, and De Vries, or on physics while ignoring Einstein, Planck, Bohr, and atomic fission. Orwell cannot be laughed off because he is primarily a novelist. Novelists and poets, men of superior imagination, have usually preceded the solemn publicists and scholars in anticipating great trends in history and thought. For example, the Roman poet Lucretius anticipated Herbert Spencer and Charles Darwin by nearly two thousand years in setting forth the conception of universal evolution. Our social scientists will ultimately catch up with Orwell if they possess sufficient courage and realism. Indeed, two have already done so. James Burnham predicted and described the military managerialism which is the essence of "Nineteen Eighty-Four" political theory and practice. John T. Flynn, in his *As We Go Marching*, revealed in trenchant fashion the ominous development of American totalitarianism based on the war spirit and psychological warfare.

Orwell was admirably prepared to write his book. He was well-trained in aristocratic English higher education. He spent some time as an English police officer in Burma, was a volunteer in the Spanish civil war, and served in an important post in the official propaganda work of the British government during the Second World War. This gave him close familiarity with contemporary propaganda methods ("emotional engineering") and the technique of public lying. His knowledge of Russian totalitarianism was made manifest in his book *Animal Farm*, an achievement in social satire which led many to compare him with Swift and Defoe. The fundamental importance of his prospectus in *Nineteen Eighty-Four* has been attested to by Bertrand Russell and other equally eminent social philosophers.

In a brief portion of this book Orwell reduces his prophecy to a relentlessly precise ideology. According to this presentation, what we have to fear is not so much state capitalism, Communism, or Fascism, but a more brutal form of totalitarianism based on perpetual war which is designed to deprive the masses of the material fruits of our advancing technology and of the leisure, education, and freedom which Bellamy believed would accompany such technological accomplishments.

Orwell points out that the political and economic leaders of this pattern of life and public order slowly developed their ideology and practical program as the result of the growing conviction that, if the people were freely granted all the advantages which might logically arise from an ever more productive material culture, they would have a greater opportunity for leisure and education and might thus develop some capacity for the rational discussion and analysis of public problems. If this should happen, the public would then demand competent and honest leadership in economic and political life, full use of our impressive technological equipment for providing consumer goods, and a better distribution of the products of our mechanical empire. In short, the new popular demands would upset the existing political and economic order and oust the chief custodians and direct beneficiaries thereof.

The problem, therefore, which faced those in control of society, as the mid-century approached, was to be able to continue our mechanization, but also to prevent its advantages and achieve-

---

[1]George Orwell, *Nineteen Eighty-Four* (New York: Harcourt, Brace and Company, Inc., 1949), pp. 185 ff.

ments from reaching and benefitting the masses in anything like a normal and unrestricted fashion. To revert to an agricultural economy would be impossible in practice today. It would reverse the whole trend of thought and of industrial evolution, and it would be suicidal for any one country to attempt such a policy in a world still dominated by the war spirit. Nor would it be possible to deprive the masses of technological benefits by deliberately and drastically restricting the output of goods. This would produce wholesale misery and discontent and would entail vast relief problems and expenses. It might even provoke widespread revolution, since there would be no compensatory fear or excitement. Wasteful "make-work"—pyramid building, CWA, and the like—would deprive the masses of the benefits of our mechanical production, but it would not keep them excited and subdued. They would become fatigued and bored, and revolt might ensue. The only solution, therefore, seemed to be to continue mechanical development, perhaps even augment it, but to destroy through a perpetual state of war all the products thereof which are not needed for the bare survival of the masses.

The leaders of the "Nineteen Eighty-Four" pattern of society were, however, sagacious enough to recognize that, if this perpetual war were a bona fide hot war, earnestly conducted with present-day instruments of mass destruction, nearly everybody on the earth would soon be destroyed. Hence, the leaders in all three great blocks of nations—Oceania (the United States, the British Empire, and Latin America), Eurasia (the U.S.S.R., Continental Europe, and the Middle East), and Eastasia (China, southeastern Asia, Oceania, and parts of Africa)—agree to keep the warfare perpetually phony. There is little or no real war. Everybody is kept feverishly busy making war machinery and munitions but these are, unknown to the masses, allowed to rust or rot and are rarely used in any actual fighting. Airplanes are flown off by the thousands and abandoned in the deserts, soon to be followed by flocks of new ones similarly destined for oblivion. Great fleets of war vessels are taken out secretly at night and sunk in the ocean and new fleets are built to meet a similar fate.

Yet this strategem can only work if the masses are always kept at a fever heat of fear and excitement and are effectively prevented from learning that the wars are actually phony. To bring about this indispensable deception of the people requires a tre-

mendous development of propaganda, thought-policing, regimentation, and mental terrorism—in short, "emotional engineering" and pyschological warfare on an overwhelming scale.
Systematic hate campaigns are developed and daily hate periods
are made compulsory. An all-pervading and most meticulous
system of espionage is maintained, even to the extent of keeping
every citizen constantly under the scrutiny of a television eye
through which those in charge of the espionage system can keep
posted with respect to every detail in the behavior and attitudes of
all citizens. Both past history and current news are constantly
falsified and rewritten to conform to the daily statements and
policies of those in charge of the regime.[2]

Indeed, a veritable semantic revolution in official phraseology
is achieved to facilitate the deception of the masses by the leaders.
A new and fitting vocabulary is provided in what Orwell calls
"Newspeak," and the orderly logic of former days is replaced by
the technique of "doublethink," which permits the wholesale acceptance and retention of directly contradictory concepts. For example, in *Nineteen Eighty-Four* the Ministry of War is called the
Ministry of Peace; the department which administers propaganda
and mass deception is designated the Ministry of Truth; all the
horrible espionage, intimidation, and tortures are carried out by
the Ministry of Love; and the responsibility for keeping the
masses both excited and yet under control, while in privation and
misery, is the task of the Ministry of Plenty.

Though there are few or no battles actually fought on the battlefield or on the seas, fake battles of vast magnitude are reported
in spectacular fashion in the newspapers, over the radio, and in
the movies and television. The masses believe that great victories
are being won, though they are told that the military situation
constantly demands their most feverish energy and loyal support
in order that they save themselves from extinction. When it
becomes impossible to keep the people any longer at a white heat
in their hatred of one enemy group of nations, the war is shifted
against another bloc and new, violent hate campaigns are planned
and set in motion. In other words, the basic public policy and political technique, within the general framework of perpetual

[2]See my "Revisionism and the Historical Blackout" [in this collection].

phony war, is what we have come to know of in our own society today as "psychological warfare."

In this manner the masses are kept disciplined and impoverished, but are also sufficiently excited and intimidated so that they do not actively resent the grim, drab, and tyrannical mode of life to which they are condemned. They are also diverted by cheap circuses, fake lotteries, and the like. All reliable historical material and all possible avenues of contact with the past are destroyed so that the masses will never become discontented or restless through being able to contrast their current unhappy estate with the blessings of life in previous generations. The leaders are thus able to maintain their dominion and tenure indefinitely and continue essentially unchallenged.

The main lesson driven home by Orwell's disconcerting book is that we face a sharp and ominous revolution in the whole nature and purpose of warfare. In the past, wars have been mainly the product of personal or partisan political ambition, emotional rage, national arrogance, or definite plans to conquer territory for glory, necessity, or both. They have been fought against a foreign enemy with all possible vigor and the best strategy then available. The enemy has been nations, parties, or forces *outside* the boundary of the countries involved. Victory has been sought as speedily as possible. And victory meant the decisive military defeat of the enemy on the battlefield. In earlier days, warfare was rarely adopted as a normal technique of domestic political strategy, though the idea is not a new one, having been forecast in the "giddy minds and foreign quarrels" formula suggested by Shakespeare in his *Henry IV*.[3]

Orwell imples that we are now passing into a period in which wars—hot, cold, or phony—are being used to an increasing extent as the basic mode of class and partisan political strategy in order to consolidate the power of the class or party in office, to extend and retain tenure of office, and to maintain full employment and avert depressions. The main enemy is not nations or forces *outside* the border but parties and classes *within* the country that are antagonistic to the party and class which holds the power.

There is no desire to defeat the alleged foreign enemy quickly

[3]Cf. Charles A. Beard, *Giddy Minds and Foreign Quarrels* (New York: The Macmillan Company, 1939).

and decisively, for to do so would curtail or end the armament industry, threaten a depression, invite social discontent, and jeopardize the existing social, economic, and political order. Wars must be prolonged as much as possible—made perpetual, in fact—so as to assure full employment and facilitate the propaganda of fear and terrorism upon which the maintenance of the regime depends. War strategy is no longer to be entrusted to vigorous military experts of the older type. It is primarily the task of the politicians, operating through propaganda and intimidation, and of political generals. The totalitarian horrors of the system which Orwell portrays are incidental to the maintenance and perpetuation of the perpetual phony warfare upon which the whole new social order is constructed.

The obvious implication is that, if we wish to avoid the establishment or continuation of such a regime as Orwell portrays, we can only succeed by attacking the new foreign policy and phony war system. No success can be attained merely by battling against incidental products and symptoms of the system, such as inroads on civil liberties, economic regimentation, thought-policing, and the like. The keystone of the menacing totalitarian trend is the interventionist foreign policy, and on that the friends of liberty, democracy, and peace must concentrate their assault if they wish to accomplish anything of permanent significance.

When Orwell's book was published it was given wide publicity, but the majority of the comment upon it was superficial and represented the book as an ill-concealed satire on conditions of life in Soviet Russia and on possible future developments in Britain, if the Labor government continued its sway. Few commentators were sufficiently discerning and sagacious to recognize that the basic pattern of public behavior portrayed, namely, using some kind of war—hot, cold, or phony—as the fundamental instrument of both political and economic policy, had become the one into which all the chief countries of the world are slipping, perhaps irrevocably, unless the trend is recognized and reversed in time.

Indeed, the prospect facing all the important nations today is far more grim than that portrayed in *Nineteen Eighty-Four,* which so horrified the majority of those who read the book. The perpetual war of "Nineteen Eighty-Four" society is strictly phony and very few lose their lives therein. Everybody is employed and secure, even though the masses are intimidated and merely subsist on an extremely low standard of living.

There seems little probability that those who are today using cold wars and war scares to remain in office, ward off a depression, and increase the power and prestige of the military caste, will be successful indefinitely in keeping all future warfare phony and relatively bloodless. The munitions that are being turned out and the new and fearful agencies of mechanized warfare are not so likely to be allowed to rot and rust or be deliberately destroyed as they are to be applied in actual processes of unparalleled destruction. Unless the trend toward war can be checked, and that soon, we face not only the mental intimidation and terrorism of "Nineteen Eighty-Four" society, but unprecedented destruction of life and property. The already famous issue of *Collier's* (October 27, 1951), on "The War We Do Not Want," predicted and portrayed the probable course, character, and results of the third world war. Though extremely optimistic as to the outcome for the United States and its allies, the picture given was completely appalling in relation to the devastation wrought.

Many have dismissed the "Nineteen Eighty-Four" pattern of life as merely a terrifying fantasy, but the literal truth is that, in all the basic essentials, it has already become well established throughout much of the world. The warring groups of *Nineteen Eighty-Four*—Oceania, Eurasia, and Eastasia—have already come into being and are rehearsing for world war in Korea, whether it turns out to be cold, hot, or phony. Orwell himself recognized this to be the fact, and Stephen Spender asserted in the *New York Times* that Orwell originally intended to entitle his book "Nineteen Forty-Eight," an idea which he abandoned only because he feared it would cause too much reader resistance and incredulity.

"Nineteen Eighty-Four" Traits in American Culture at the Mid-Century

It is obvious that we have already gone far along the line of "Nineteen Eighty-Four" trends in the United States, and all current evidence suggests that we shall continue to pursue them. As we have pointed out, our "prosperity," since 1940, has been based upon a war and quasi-war economy. As Norman Thomas well said: "If the Lord should send the Angel Gabriel to the world with the announcement that the Diety had forbidden all further wars, we would at once enter the greatest depression of our history." Our leading "court economist," Sumner H. Schlichter, has frequently given his blessing to the cold war as an effective means of warding off depressions and assuring the continuance of American "prosperity." Others have followed suit. In a penetrating column in the *New York Herald Tribune* for April 7, 1952, David Lawrence emphasized the dominant influence of the cold war and of armament expenditures in creating and perpetuating American economic prosperity. He stressed the alarming prospect of a serious depression, even a panic, in case pacific relations between the United States and Russia developed to such an extent as to cause an abandonment of a vast spending program for armaments. Lawrence warned that we must take steps to prepare ourselves against the economic disaster of a "sudden peace." Hot and cold wars have kept the Democrats in power since 1939, and they promise to continue to do so indefinitely, especially if a hot war breaks out.

When we spend over 90 percent of our federal budget for wars, past, present, and future, we have already taken great strides toward depriving the masses of the benefits of our more profuse mechanical production. The Point Four program imposes only a planetary limit on current and future "operations rathole." Indeed, there would be no assurance that we would end the cold war and "Nineteen Eighty-Four" patterns, even though the United States and its allies completely subdued the whole planet. In this age of rockets and stratosphere cruising, globaloney could easily be supplanted by "astrobaloney," and the masses could be intimidated by fear of invasion from other planets. Kenneth Heuer has already written a thrilling, quasi-factual book on *Men of Other Planets* which could readily be exploited by our Ministries of Peace and Truth in the cause of astrobaloney and to procure lavish outlays for aid to Mars and Mercury as a defense against possible invasion from Jupiter and Saturn.[4] That there is nothing fan-

---

[4]New York: Pellegrini and Cudahy, 1951. See also the article in *Time*, April 14, 1952, on the apparently serious program of Lancelot Hogben and the British Interplanetary Society to establish promptly interplanetary radio communication.

ciful about predicting a future era of astrobaloney is demonstrated by the national panic generated by Orson Welles's purely fake broadcast of an invasion from Mars on October 30, 1938. The newspapers on the next morning asserted that a "tidal wave of terror swept the nation." What might take place, as mechanization and propaganda techniques improve, defies the imagination.

The most characteristic and conspicuous trait of "Nineteen Eighty-Four" policy is the fact that every public measure, whether military outlays, propaganda programs, intimidation, witchhunting, tortures, or oppression of the masses, is justified on the ground that it is essential to security and *defense* against the enemy. The amazing and alarming development of the same technique in the United States, is, perhaps, the most convincing evidence of the extent to which we have adopted the Orwell pattern. The War Department has disappeared; instead, we now have a Department of Defense. War is not quite yet Peace, but it *has* become Defense. Our astronomical military budget, basic political policies, security measures, witch-hunting, loyalty tests—indeed, every extraordinary public action, is justified on the ground that it is absolutely essential to defense. Policies and acts which would be repudiated instantly under any other circumstances can be promoted, and usually accomplished, if it can be successfully alleged that they are vitally related to the defense program. Even those who attack the official policy are successful to the extent that they can demonstrate that they are speaking and acting in behalf of more adequate defense. There has been no more sincere effort than there is in *Nineteen Eighty-Four* to examine the actual need for, or validity of, the defense program.

The doublethink in the whole defense propaganda is readily apparent from the obvious fact that the Russia which is now portrayed as about to spring at the world and devour it is the same Russia that Roosevelt, Harry Hopkins, and other administration leaders presented to the American public as our must potent and suitable ally in the global struggle to suppress totalitarianism, assure democracy, promote liberty, and make peace secure throughout the world. There is very little today in Russian policy, domestic or foreign, which any informed person did not know about back in 1941. In fact, nothing which Russia has done since 1945 has been as aggressive and brutal as the invasion of Poland in the autumn of 1939, the later mass murders of Polish officers in the Katyn Forest in 1940, or the mass murders and deportations of Baltic peoples during the war. Russian zest for territorial gains along her border was made amply manifest in Poland, during the wartime conferences, and elsewhere before August 1945.

The fact that President Truman launched his Truman Doctrine and the cold war without being motivated by any marked change in the character of Russia is emphasized by the following evidence. On February 28, 1947, Mr. Truman wrote a letter to ex-Governor George H. Earle of Pennsylvania, who was at the time a leading Russophobe and alarmist relative to the menace of Russian and Communist aggression. President Truman counselled moderation. He stated that he did not believe that there was any serious menace from Communism. There were few Communists in the United States, and the American people were too prosperous and sensible to be susceptible to Communist propaganda. The implications of the letter were that the ex-governor would do well to taper off his alarmism. But just twelve days later Mr. Truman went before Congress and announced his Truman Doctrine and cold-war policy, maintaining that the peace of the world and the safety of the United States depended on checking the Soviet and Communist menace. It is quite obvious that Soviet Russia and its ideology had undergone no marked changes in these twelve days. What had happened was that Britain had recently announced her support of Greece and Turkey. Clark Clifford and other astute political advisers of the president saw in this an opportunity to rehabilitate Mr. Truman's fast-fading political prospects.

The hate campaign, so terrifyingly portrayed in *Nineteen Eighty-Four*, is well under way against Soviet Russia, Communist China, and the ''Reds'' generally. So, also, is the thought-policing, assailed by Bernard De Voto in *Harper's*, October, 1949 and made the subject of four recent books: Walter Gellhorn's *Security, Loyalty and Science*, Max Lowenthal's *The Federal Bureau of Investigation*, Carey McWilliams's *Witch Hunt*, and Francis Biddle's *The Fear of Freedom*.

In no respect is the ''doublethink'' in our emergent ''Nineteen Eighty-Four'' system more flagrantly apparent than with respect to civil liberties. President Truman has made the promotion of civil liberties more of an administration issue than any other president. That he is sincere about it is proved by the fact that he has been willing to violate political expediency to forward this program, something almost unique in his policy, even to the extent of producing a bolt from the democratic party in the South. Yet, at the same time, the Truman Doctrine, the cold war, and the alleged security needs that have resulted, have been almost the sole reason for the recent invasion of our traditional civil liberties which are beyond precedent in all American history since 1789.

Two Supreme Court decisions in 1947 and 1950 destroyed a vital cornerstone of our basic civil liberties—that which guarantees us freedom from the search of our homes and offices without a search warrant.[5] This was a right demanded by the English pioneers of civil liberty in their battles against Stuart tyranny in the seventeenth century and by our colonial forefathers in their struggles for liberty on the eve of the American Revolution. It was supposed to be firmly secured by the Fourth Amendment. Its elimination opens the way to just the type of totalitarian snooping and invasion of privacy which prevails in "Nineteen Eighty-Four" society. It is characteristic of the new or "totalitarian liberalism" that the 1950 decision was written by Justice Sherman Minton, at one time one of the most ardent supporters of the New Deal.

The drastic legislation recently passed to suppress radicalism, the reactionary decisions by distinguished erstwhile liberal judges in the federal courts, such as Learned Hand, indicate that the raid on our civil liberties has only just begun to get under way. President Truman's much publicized civil rights program may turn out to be no more than the privilege of minority groups to share with the majority the mutual surrender of our traditional civil liberties. The Smith Act of June 28, 1940, finally upheld by an impressive majority of the Supreme Court, repudiated the fundamental principles on which our nation was founded and outlawed what Abraham Lincoln held in his first inaugural address to be the "most sacred right of mankind." Not only Jefferson and Patrick Henry, but John Adams and Alexander Hamilton, could be thrown into prison if they were alive today and gave vent to the views they expressed while living.[6] Though the Smith Act is now being used to

---

[5]*Harris* v. *U.S.*, 331 U.S. 145, 1947; and *U.S.* v. *Rabinowitz*, 339 U.S. 56, 1950. The Supreme Court has upheld search without warrant in some eleven other cases, although some of them were simply on the basis of a denial of certiorari.

[6]H. E. Barnes, *History and Social Intelligence* (New York: Alfred A. Knopf, 1926), pp. 314–28.

suppress the vending of unpopular Communist opinions, it could readily be turned against the very conservative groups that have sponsored the law, if radicals ever obtain control over our government.

How dangerous it is for one group or class to initiate a legislative witch-hunting crusade against another is well illustrated by changes since 1944. In that year the totalitarian liberals, fellow travelers, and Communists invoked the Smith Act against alleged pro-Fascists in the mass sedition trial. Within less than five years the same law was being turned against the very groups that sought, with such glee and gusto, to use it to suppress their opponents in 1944.

President Truman denounced the McCarran Act of 1950 as destructive of our civil liberties, but this law was only a logical outcome and byproduct of the Truman Doctrine. There is not the slightest possibility that such a bill would even have been introduced had not President Truman launched the cold war as a desperate act of political expediency.[7]

We have thus far remained content to arrest and convict Communists, for the Socialists are now impotent, and there is little point in arresting Republicans so long as leaders in the Republican party heartily support the "Nineteen Eighty-Four" trends that keep the Democrats in power. Republicans like the late Arthur H. Vandenberg, Warren R. Austin, Irving M. Ives, Henry Cabot Lodge, John Foster Dulles, Harold E. Stassen, Leverett Saltonstall, James H. Duff, Thomas E. Dewey, and Wayne L. Morse are worth more politically to the Democrats than the whole Democratic National Committee. If we enter a depression and things tighten up, it may be quite a different story.

The censorship of higher education, well illustrated by conditions and developments at the University of Washington, the University of California, and at Ohio State University, demonstrates how "Nineteen Eighty-Four" trends are permeating our educational institutions and bringing them into conformity with our "Ministry of Truth." These trends are reminiscent of the ear-

[7]For a summary of the inroads on our civil liberties produced by the cold war, see Clair Wilcox, ed., *Civil Liberties Under Attack* (Philadelphia: University of Pennsylvania Press, 1951); E. E. Palmer, ed., *The Communist Problem in America* (New York: Thomas Y. Crowell Company, 1951); and Francis Biddle, *The Fear of Freedom* (Garden City, N.Y.: Doubleday & Company, Inc., 1951).

ly stages of Nazi control over German universities and of the Communist sway over institutions of higher learning in the Soviet Union.

While there has already been plenty of witch-hunting carried on by our "Ministry of Love," the latter has not gone very far as yet in setting up the torture chambers so graphically described by Orwell. Most of the torture thus far administrated to dissenters has been carried out by local police through their traditional third-degree tactics. Nevertheless, once conditions demand brutality, one may be sure that our "Ministry of Love" will not fail to live up to the standards set forth by Orwell. Indeed, it will probably far surpass these. As Stewart H. Holbrook and others have done well to point out, no other civilized nation has been as prone to violence and brutality as the United States. An Englishman such as Orwell, in all probability, could not really fathom our resources or ingenuity in this field of operations.

We pointed out above that the masses in *Nineteen Eighty-Four* are diverted and distracted, in an effort to keep them from rebellion against their drab and austere living conditions, by cheap circuses, fake lotteries, and the like. We have already gone far in providing the American people with analogous entertainment. If we do not conduct fake public lotteries, we at least conduct quasi-fake public investigations of private lotteries and give these the character of circuses by television, radio, the movies, and other mass-communication devices. Gambling with slot and pinball machines seems to be a crime, while gambling with the lives of millions of Americans appears to be the essence of statecraft and the proof of public virtue.

In the first essay in this book it was pointed out how difficult it is to get any material before the public which might reveal the true facts and check the trend toward the "Nineteen Eighty-Four" pattern of life, even though our ignorance is as yet caused mainly by what Harold Ickes once called "voluntary servitude." In this respect we are worse off than those in *Nineteen Eighty-Four*, where it is represented as necessary to hire and intimidate servile bureaucrats to falsify history and to distort, select, and censor current news. In the United States today, many of our most eminent historians and most of our newspapers and radio and television stations are effectively performing this function quite voluntarily and mostly without direct expense to the government.

The hysterical reaction following Orson Welles's bogus radio broadcast on October 30, 1938, depicting an invasion from Mars, emphasizes the American capacity for credulity and shows how American wartime propaganda in the next war, whether cold, hot, or phony, can duplicate anything of the kind portrayed in *Nineteen Eighty-Four*. Those who are skeptical on this point will do well to read Hadley Cantril's book *The Invasion from Mars*.[8]

The fact that, despite an appalling mass of factual material which would logically justify greater disillusionment than that which followed the First World War and which calls for a sharp reversal of our foreign policy, our propaganda agencies have been able to perpetuate the mental attitude and policies of wartime almost intact for seven years since V-J Day, affords convincing proof that our propaganda facilities are about as powerful as those depicted in *Nineteen Eighty-Four*. Even there, a period of five to seven years is about as long as public hatred can be effectively maintained against any single group of enemy powers.

A main purpose of political propaganda in the United States is to beget and perpetuate popular fear of Russian aggression. John Foster Dulles has explained that the American people need to be "artificially alarmed" lest there be a relaxation of this fear. Senator Ralph E. Flanders has described, in part, how this fear is generated and spread from Washington:

> Fear is felt and spread by the Department of Defense in the Pentagon. In part, the spreading of it is purposeful. Faced with what seem to be enormous armed forces aimed at us, we can scarcely expect the Department of Defense to do other than to keep the people in a state of fear so that they will be prepared without limit to furnish men and munitions.... Another center from which fear is spread throughout our people is the State Department. Our diplomacy has gone on the defensive. The real dependence of the State Department is in arms, armies and allies. There is no confidence left in anything except force. The fearfulness of the Pentagon and that of the State Department complement and reinforce each other.[9]

As Garet Garret proceeds to observe: "Fear at last assumes the phase of a patriotic obsession. It is stronger than any political par-

---

[8]Princeton, N.J.: Princeton University Press, 1940.
[9]*The Freeman,* April 21, 1952, p. 470.

ty. Any candidate for office who trifles with its basic conviction
will be scourged."[10]

The synthetic and artificial nature of the fear of Russian aggression and military action is daily made more apparent. Even leading Russophobes like Eugene Lyons frankly admit that there is
every reason to expect that Russia will not start a war. Lyons embodied his predictions in an article in the *Cosmopolitan* for March
1952 entitled "Ten Reasons Why Russia Won't Fight." His
arguments and facts were convincing. The leading article in the
U.S. News and World Report for April 18, 1952, came to the same
general conclusion as that reached by Lyons. Perhaps the most
striking instance of doublethink in the artificial alarmism was
presented in the testimony of General Alfred M. Gruenther,
General Eisenhower's chief of staff, before the House Foreign
Affairs Committee on March 25, 1952: Gruenther argued vigorously that American billions must be spent in Europe for protection against Russia, but when pinned down conceded that he did
not believe the Russians will start a war, now or at any time.

"When will the attack come?" asked Representative Eaton
[Rep., N.J.].

"I don't think it is ever going to come," Gruenther replied. "I
am not one of those who subscribe to the theory of the inevitability
of war.

"I don't think that war is imminent now, and I don't think it is
ever going to come."

Such material reveals the fact that the cold war of today is even
more phony and synthetic than the phony war of *Nineteen Eighty-
Four*. In the latter the vast expenditures for war can only be produced by alarmist statements that the war is actually in progress
and that veritable extermination threatens the populations unless
they work feverishly to repel the potential invader. The frantic efforts of the interventionists to prevent the populace from grasping
the realities were well exemplified by the persistent attempt to
discredit and ridicule the Russian peace and trade gestures made
in April 1952.

The governing bureaucracy of *Nineteen Eighty-Four*, as pictured by Orwell, is made up of the very groups who are now con-
trolling American public policy: "Bureaucrats, scientists, techni-

[10]*Ibid.*

cians, journalists and professional politicians...whose origins lay in the salaried middle class and the upper grades of the working class....As compared with their opposite numbers in past ages, they were less avaricious, less tempted by luxury, hungrier for pure power, and, above all, more conscious of what they were doing and more intent on crushing opposition.''

It will be evident to discerning readers that the groups which Orwell describes are precisely our totalitarian liberals—Schlesinger, Jr.'s, ''Vital Center''—who have been taking over power since 1933 and especially since 1939. It is interesting and significant that, in its issue of February 19, 1950, the *New York Times* published a realistic survey of our current ''government types,'' which fully confirms this diagnosis of our present-day ''public servants.''

Who will become the American ''Big Brother''—the Fuehrer of our ''Nineteen Eighty-Four'' public order—is anybody's guess, but of one thing we may be certain. He will not be drawn from conservative or radical ranks. Conservative totalitarianism has been effectively smeared, and the radicals have been forced underground. Our ''Big Brother'' will be drawn from the totalitarian liberal group and will be somebody who has fervently crusaded in public in behalf of world freedom. All current trends bear out the accuracy of the late Huey Long's prediction that totalitarianism will come to the United States in the guise of anti-totalitarianism.

In an earlier version of this material the writer suggested Senator Paul H. Douglas as the most likely candidate for our American Big Brother. Historians and publicists who read this offered other favorite candidates, such as Senators Hubert H. Humphrey and Wayne L. Morse, Harold E. Stassen and Henry A. Wallace, as good choices. But the writer clings to the conviction that Senator Douglas remains the most appropriate nominee for the post. Probably no other American public figure today has shown such energy, talent for recognizing the advantages of political expediency, ethical pliability, and complete mastery of all the knowledge and requirements essential to operating the great ''Nineteen Eighty-Four'' Ministries of Peace, Truth, Love, and Plenty.

As for the ''bible'' of the developing ''Nineteen Eighty-Four'' regime in the United States, it is too early to be dogmatic. Thus far, the book which most nearly qualifies is Arthur M. Schlesinger, Jr.'s, *The Vital Center*, a clever example of totalitarian liberal "Newspeak" and "doublethink" ostensibly directed against totalitarian trends.[11] A preliminary dictionary of "Newspeak" has been prepared, apparently quite innocently, by Julien Cornell, called *New World Primer* (1947). At any rate, there is no doubt that we shall, when it is needed, be able to provide the analogue of Emmanuel Goldstein's *Theory and Practice of Oligarchical Collectivism*, the guiding manual of "Nineteen Eighty-Four" ideology and civil practice. A perfect historical introduction for such a book has already been provided by Frank Tannenbaum in his article on "The American Tradition in Foreign Relations" in *Foreign Affairs*, October 1951. Surely, the capacity of the totalitarian liberals for doublethink is already unlimited. In a book on *Civil Liberties under Attack*, edited by Clair Wilcox, criticizing the recent witch-hunting, some of the collaborators are such warmongering historians and publicists as Henry Steele Commager who have, from its inception, ardently supported the interventionist foreign policy which is almost solely responsible for the recent inroads on our liberties. Another warm supporter of Roosevelt foreign policy, Francis Biddle, who as Attorney General sanctioned the notorious mass sedition trial, deplores the witch-hunting excesses now carried on allegedly in behalf of security and defense.[12] Mr. Biddle and the Americans for Democratic Action, a leading organization of totalitarian liberals, have launched a nationwide campaign to repeal the Smith Act, now that it is being successfully applied to the conviction of Communists. But it was under this very act that Mr. Biddle instituted the mass sedition trial in 1944 against alleged Fascist and Nazi sympathizers.

The eagerness with which we may expect the totalitarian liberals to support war hysteria and the most extreme measures of propaganda was forecast when, on October 6, 1950, the Public Affairs Committee of Freedom House demanded drastic full mobilization, recommended lavish rearmament as "the major hope for peace in the world," and stated that any relaxation of mobilization would be "the most dangerous misreading of the popular mind."

[11] Boston: Houghton Mifflin Company, 1949.
[12] *The Fear of Freedom* (New York: Doubleday and Company, Inc., 1951).

The Committee on the Present Danger, the spearhead of private and quasi-official alarmist propaganda, is manned overwhelmingly by totalitarian liberals, and it is significant that it is headed by President James Bryant Conant of Harvard University, our leading totalitarian liberal educator. Conant, incidentally, has outdone even the Pentagon in vociferous advocacy of universal military training.

We have already richly developed "Newspeak" and the "doublethink" semantics of *Nineteen Eighty-Four*. Witness such popular assumptions and slogans as: War, waste, and inflation spell prosperity. Double prices and we double actual national income. National prosperity may be assured by giving away to foreign nations vast quantities of money and goods, to be paid for by the American taxpayer. Our great national debt is a blessing in disguise because we owe it to ourselves. We are setting up a welfare state by spending less than 3 percent of the federal budget for welfare. Cold war is peace. The United Nations organization, split right down through the middle by the cold war, is still united and the hope of the world. "Peaceloving nations" are nations which made war between 1939 and 1945. A "free nation" is any nation—whether liberal and democratic, socialist, fascist, or anti-Kremlin communist—which will join the anti-Russian crusade. Aiding socialist nations of Europe under the Marshall Plan is a bold stroke to promote free enterprise abroad. Bolstering the confirmed Communist Tito promotes the American way of life across the sea. The surest road to perpetual peace is through perpetual war. Launching an atom bomb race will assure peace and security. Freedom and liberty can best be guaranteed and encouraged throughout the world by first destroying our own Bill of Rights and then by setting up here at home the totalitarian methods of intimidation and witch-hunting. The best way to discourage the principle of militarism in the world is to militarize ourselves rapidly and completely and to indoctrinate our youth with military ideals.

One could continue this list almost indefinitely, but the above examples will be sufficient to drive home the point that our public opinion is now being overwhelmingly shaped by doublethink and the related semantic ruses so familiar to readers of *Nineteen Eighty-Four*.

Intellectual, political, and military trends since the Korean war broke out confirm Orwell's thesis as to wartime behavior in the future. If words mean anything, it would seem that our basic policy in the Korean adventure is to prolong the struggle as much as possible. On July 23, 1951, Secretary of State Dean Acheson asserted: "If anything is important, if anything is true about the situation in Korea, it is the overwhelming importance of not forcing a showdown on our side in Korea and not permitting our opponents to force a showdown."

We have already referred to the precipitate demand for drastic mobilization by one of our most prominent totalitarian liberal organizations. President Truman's emergency proclamation of December 16, 1951, may fairly be regarded as the formal installation of our "Nineteen Eighty-Four" regime. The Psychological Strategy Board, which was set up soon afterward with Gordon Gray as its head, was the first long step in creating our "Ministry of Truth." It was designed to "provide for the more effective planning, coordination and conduct, within the framework of approved national policies, of psychological operations"—in short, to launch a vast program of psychological warfare, the most characteristic public operation in *Nineteen Eighty-Four*. What has been accomplished here, down to 1952, was well described by Anthony Leviero in a series of articles in the *New York Times* during the week of December 10, 1951.

The mystery-shrouded war news reminiscent of *Nineteen Eighty-Four*, and the vagueness on the home front as to where the fighting is really taking place and who is winning, have also been leading traits of war publicity and popular reactions relative to the Korean War. The heating and cooling off of the war, which has repeatedly occurred since June 1950 are reminiscent of Orwell's description of war in *Nineteen Eighty-Four*, as also are the headline reports that the great majority of the casualties are suffered by the enemy. So are the series of disclosures of "atrocities," often in regular patterns, and sometimes long after the alleged incidents have occurred. It was stated that newsmen had been barred from the mass executions which featured the return of Syngman Rhee to his beloved native land so as to reinstate democracy there. Rhee, who fled his country for many years, was repudiated in the popular elections months before the outbreak of the Korean war, and had maintained his tenure by totalitarian methods, has been widely proclaimed "the George Washington of Korea."

The MacArthur controversy cannot be understood in any fundamental way except in terms of "Nineteen Eighty-Four" concepts. Both MacArthur and Truman were right and logical in the light of their sharply contrasting assumptions.

General MacArthur thought in terms of the traditional soldier, who believed in fighting an all-out military war against a foreign enemy who should be defeated or destroyed as soon as possible and by sound strategic methods. Within this framework of thought the only victory is a military victory, and, indeed, there can be no substitute for it. In the light of such assumptions, MacArthur's proposals made complete sense and his exasperation with President Truman and Secretary Acheson was fully justified. What he did not understand was that war had been transformed and is now governed by "Nineteen Eighty-Four" considerations instead of by traditional military philosophy and strategy.

President Truman and his advisers were fighting the limited (phony) war of the "Nineteen Eighty-Four" pattern. A foreign nation is an enemy only in formal fiction today. The real enemy is forces and factors within the boundaries of the nation itself—partisan or class competition and economic depression. In such a war, the president and his party were winning a "victory" every day at home, even when our forces were being temporarily routed in Korea. So long as Democratic tenure seemed assured and the depression was postponed, victory was constantly at hand. The worst possible defeat would have been a quick and decisive military victory over the North Koreans and the Chinese. This would have ended the emergency, weakened the Democrats, undermined lavish defense expenditures, and threatened us with abysmal depression.

This "Nineteen Eighty-Four" type of permanent victory was hardly one which an old-line soldier like MacArthur could comprehend. His dismissal brought to an end, for the time being at least, an epoch of military history and patterns which had endured for at least six thousand years. It was Truman's misfortune to have had a traditional soldier in command in the Far East. All would have gone smoothly if he could have entrusted the Korean command from the onset to one of his Pentagon generals who fully understood the transformation in the nature and motivation of warfare that had taken place since V-J Day. However, General MacArthur's alert and powerful mind enabled him to educate himself rapidly as to the real nature of our policy in the cold war and in the Korean conflict. In his speech before the Michigan legislature on May 15, 1952, he showed himself fully aware of the "Nineteen Eighty-Four" character of our current foreign and military policy.

The long and tortuous discussions during the cease-fire negotiations in Korea, the numerous clashes over relative trivialities, the endless delays, the frequent breakoff of negotiations, and the seeming reluctance to effect a real and sincere truce, were all evidences of the aversion of both sides to terminate hostilities in the limited war. President Truman's indignation over a mistaken order to cease all hostilities for even a day underlined his fear of any immediate pacific outcome. It is unquestionably true that nothing else in American or world policy today smacks quite as much of "Nineteen Eighty-Four" mental and political attitudes as the Korean armistice negotiations.

The declining public interest in the Korean war has made President Truman and his associates the more willing to accept Churchill's proposal to shift the main psychological impact of the cold war to Indochina, where it may both revive flagging American fear and excitement and also more directly protect adjacent British interests. The Orwell formula has been faithfully worked out in first directing fear and hatred against Nazi Germany, then against Soviet Russia, next shifting antagonism more toward Communist China, and then moving the chief center of interest in the struggle against the latter from Korea to Indochina.

There has been much talk about the danger of direct military dictatorship over the United States. It has been seriously reported that, despite the fact that we recently fought a war against Nazi militarism, the top Army officials in the Pentagon have taken over a plan for the mobilization of the United States written by one of Hitler's generals. Nevertheless, in a long and scholarly book on *American Democracy and Military Power*,[13] Dean Louis Smith of the University of Chicago has recently made it clear that our past history, even of the Second World War, affords little basis for any such fear in the immediate future. Warmongering, war hysteria, and excesses against civil liberties and personal rights have invariably been due to the panic and sadism of civil authorities. If the latter retain sanity and really seek peace, there is little need to fear military dictatorship.

13Chicago: University of Chicago Press, 1951.

The Principal Nations of the World Have Slipped into the "Nineteen Eighty-Four" Pattern

Some who agree with much of the preceding material will, nevertheless, raise their hands in horror and maintain stoutly that Americans will never permit such a development to take place here. The most cogent answer to this is that it has already happened in all basic essentials, without more than a handful of Americans realizing it. The developments have all been camouflaged behind a deceptive blanket of pseudo-libertarian "Newspeak." If the trend moves on as rapidly and inexorably after 1952 as it has from 1937 to 1952, we shall have achieved the "Nineteen Eighty-Four" pattern completely, long before 1984, with only such variations in details as special circumstances and American culture produce.

Despite the fact that all the chief civilized nations have already entered to a dangerous extent into a pattern of life in which both political strategy and business policy are linked to a relatively permanent and expanding war economy, this has rarely been the product of any consciously elaborated and closely reasoned ideology, such as that portrayed by Orwell in the philosophic sections of his book.[14] It has gradually developed, mainly as a result of opportunism, a favoring chain of circumstances, and the logic of events. Though all the principal nations are converging upon the same pattern, the motivation and initial developments have differed among the various countries.

Soviet Russia was diverted from using the advantages of technology for the benefit of the masses as a result of the challenge of Hitler, the Second World War, and threats of attack thereafter. Following 1933, and especially after 1936, the Soviet Five Year Plans were concentrated more and more on the production of capital goods and armaments at the expense of consumer-goods production. Even before the rise of Hitler, Soviet Russia had fully established a system of psychological warfare, thought control, and espionage as a phase of revolutionary techniques and totalitarian policy. Its Ministries of "Love" and "Truth" had preceded the coming of the Nazis.

[14]See Orwell, *op. cit.,* pp. 185 ff.

Britain was led into the "Nineteen Eighty-Four" pattern primarily because of the political ambition of Winston Churchill and the antagonism of the Labor party to Nazism. Churchill quite correctly understood that he could not realize his lifelong ambition to become Prime Minister except in the event of a war crisis. There is no evidence that he was, personally, bitterly antagonistic to conservative totalitarian ways or really fearful that Hitler might conquer Britain. He praised Mussolini as probably the greatest statesman of the twentieth century and frequently expressed admiration for Hitler. Indeed, as late as Armistice Day, 1938, Churchill gave voice to the wish that Britain might find her Hitler in case she came into the same sorry state in which Germany had found itself by 1932.

The British Labor party, which had been whipped into a fury of hatred of Nazism by Harold Laski and others, was as enthusiastic for war in 1939 as Churchill. Hence, when it came into power in 1945, it could not repudiate the militant spirit. It was drawn into the cold war, first suggested by Churchill at Fulton, Missouri, in 1946, because of its dependence upon American financial aid, which would not have been forthcoming to a neutral and pacific Britain.

Churchill may well have recommended the cold war in the thought that its development and ramifications might return him to office as Prime Minister. At any event, it has had this result. It was the adoption of the cold-war program which so handicapped the Labor government that its record in the postwar years enabled Mr. Churchill to defeat it in the election of 1951 and once more assume the mantle of Prime Minister. But the situation has backfired on Churchill, and his political triumph in the autumn of 1951 has already proved a Pyrrhic victory. England, by seeking to rearm extensively under the cold-war pattern, became so impoverished that, six years after his Fulton speech, Churchill came to the United States with a tin cup in his hand, seeking in a plaintive mood to find some practical way of mitigating the cold war.

In this country we entered the war pattern after 1937, when political and economic opposition paralyzed the New Deal and led President Roosevelt to believe that armament and war presented the only means of assuring the perpetuation of Democratic tenure.[15] This saved the day from 1939 to early 1947, when the Demo-

---

[15]See Frederic R. Sanborn, *Design for War* (New York: The Devin-Adair Co., 1951), Chap. III.

crats seemed to be facing more or less certain defeat in 1948. At this crucial political moment, President Truman launched the cold war and saved his party, with the aid of the inept bipartisan foreign policy of powerful Republican leaders headed by Senator Arthur H. Vandenberg and John Foster Dulles. Both Democrats and Republican bipartisans were warmly supported by the official peace movement and the internationalists, by this time thoroughly converted to global meddling and "perpetual war for perpetual peace." The cold war, thus initiated by the United States with Churchill's inspiration, was sold to the Western European nations on the Continent as the price they had to pay for relief from the economic shock of war and its accompanying destruction.

Communist China was led into the cold war as an inevitable accompaniment of American diplomacy and military policy after 1945, and directly by the intervention of the United States in the Korean war in 1950.

All these groups of nations involved in the cold war, with the possible exception of Great Britain, appear highly pleased for the time being with the emergence of this new pattern of life and public policy. In the United States it won the election of 1948 for the Democratic party and seems likely to perpetuate its tenure indefinitely. Even if the Republicans should win the election in 1952, it might make little difference with respect to the continuance of the "Nineteen Eighty-Four" trend. The bipartisan Republicans are apparently powerful enough to prevent any Republican candidate from being nominated and from campaigning on the platform of a return to traditional American neutrality. Indeed, most Republican criticism of President Truman has been based on the contention that he has not been vigorous enough in his war program. The Western European nations in the Atlantic Pact or NATO lineup are congenial to the cold-war pattern because it insures for them indefinite continuance of American bounty and charity.

Stalin and his associates are highly content with the cold war because war scares and the alleged threat of capitalistic attack enable the Politburo to maintain unity in Soviet Russia, despite much brutal slave labor and low living standards. It also aids Stalin and his associates in cementing the cordon of satellite countries much more closely and firmly to the Soviet Union, and in assuring unity with Communist China and the revolutionary forces throughout Asia. The Russians also believe that they are winning the cold war.

The Chinese Communists have every reason to feel highly pleased with the institution and continuation of the cold war. It has notably assisted them in their conquest of China. It has enabled them to concentrate their power and to consolidate their gains. The antagonism of the Western Powers and the Korean war have aided them in instituting a reign of terror and in eliminating their enemies under the guise of the needs of defense and national security. The Korean war has also provided the Chinese with Russian technological and military aid and has given them indispensable training in mechanized warfare, especially military aviation. Terroristic executions and war losses are no deterrent to them, for these only help to solve the Chinese problem of excessive population. There is every evidence that not only Communist China but all of "Eastasia" is very congenial to the cold-war system, for it encourages and aids their rebellion against Western imperialism. The same is obviously true of the Middle East and Africa.

Nevertheless, no matter how well satisfied all existing parties to the cold war may be at the moment, no discerning observer of world affairs can feel very contented or reassured regarding such developments. They may produce temporary economic prosperity, promote national unity, and prolong political tenure, but they also threaten the very foundations of civilization. A cold war cannot be continued indefinitely unless it is made warmer and warmer. And the warmer it becomes, the greater the probability that it will break out into a hot war. The latter, if it comes and is fought even with the impressive weapons of destruction already available, is not only bound to wreck the economic life of the world but is all too likely to uproot what remains of all human decency and civilization. Never before have politicians, military leaders, and business forces played so lightheartedly and ruthlessly with as dangerous a toy as the cold war of our time or the "limited war" in Korea, Indochina, and elsewhere.

How the Cold-War Pattern Developed
in the United States

We have already made it clear that the cold-war pattern which dominates the world today is, in part, an opportunist affair and has not been the product of any carefully thought-out program, developed over many years of deliberate discussion and philosophical formulation. This is especially true of the practical party politicians in the United States.

Many of the most powerful politicians in the United States would probably not even know the meaning of such abstruse phraseology as Orwell's statement about "depriving the masses of the fruits of an ever-expanding technology." They would probably only register a mental and facial blank as a response to such a phrase. But, whatever their ideological innocence and poverty, they are clever politicians.

They have learned through years of experience that any proposal to spend money for the promotion of American prosperity and well-being at home is immediately branded as "Socialism" and loses for its sponsor both prestige and votes. On the other hand, a demand for limitless financial support, based on war scares and witch hunts, will produce billions in appropriations and insure enhanced political popularity. Hence, in a short time, the politicians "caught on" and now operate according to the Orwell formula, though most of them have never heard of Orwell's book and many of them would not understand its basic import, even if somebody endeavored to explain it to them at some length and with much care. Domestic welfare programs have become mainly phony, even if the cold war cannot, assuredly, be maintained forever on a phony basis. Even a man like President Truman, who is undoubtedly a kindly man and wishes the human race well, asked for only 6 percent of the federal budget for welfare purposes, and this trivial demand was curtailed by congressional hostility and penury at the very time when Congress granted the president nearly a billion dollars more than he asked for in his lavish armament program. Welfare appropriations are cut to the bone while the military forces are provided with $95 billion to spend, if they can, during the next year.

Also, opportunism obviously dominates the reactions of the military officers—army, navy, and air—in the Department of Defense. They are as innocent as the politicians about depriving the masses of the fruits of an advancing technology. What the military know is that they are having thrown at them power and funds beyond their wildest dreams, and they are quite naturally and justly making hay while the sun shines. Opportunism and naive ideology are merged in the case of starry-eyed and truly idealistic internationalists. They would seem to be mainly the product of long indoctrination with globaloney rather than sinister conspirators who have consciously recognized the value to them of the Orwellian pattern of life and policy.

But there is one powerful group whose attitudes and policies are not opportunistic or hastily pulled together. The rise of globaloney, world-meddling, and perpetual war against aggressors presents one of the most impressive examples of doublethink in human experience. The hard core and prime influence in this trend is the official and organized peace movement. Originally, this group strongly favored actual peace, neutrality, and the utmost possible limitation of warfare. But it was captured for war to end war following 1914, mainly through the efforts of the Carnegie Endowment for International Peace, and it later lined up behind the League of Nations. Having become enlisted in behalf of such premature plans of world government, it inevitably gave support to that global policing which, as John Bassett Moore warned, is now transforming every border clash into a world war.

A number of elements, forces, and policies have contributed to shape and strengthen this ominous development. One was the sanctions policy and machinery of the League of Nations. Another was the fiction of "aggressive war" and "aggressor nations" invented by James T. Shotwell and others. This fantasy was furthered through a distortion of the futile Kellogg Peace Pact by Henry L. Stimson, who held that wars had been outlawed by the pact, and, hence, any nation which made war was an outlaw and an aggressor. He combined this with the sanctions doctrine and sought to apply it against Japan. Blocked from taking extreme measures with his dangerous illusion by President Hoover, Stimson was able to sell his formula to President-elect Roosevelt in January 1933. Roosevelt, Hull, and later Stimson himself employed this diplomatic doctrine to maneuver Japan into war in December 1941. The idea was kept alive during the war and was revived thereafter by Dean Acheson, a loyal disciple of Stimson and a warm admirer of his diplomatic precepts. Acheson and his associates have thus been able to provide an ideological basis for the Truman Doctrine, which was originally adopted in haste as an act of desperate political expediency. In this way it has developed into a well-planned crusade, conducted with all the ruthless vigor characteristic of the rulers in *Nineteen Eighty-Four.*[16]

The case of President Truman in relation to all this is a complicated matter. At the beginning his action was purely that of a shrewd politician, innocent of world affairs and of any decisive diplomatic ideology. As time has gone on there is no doubt that he has been affected by the ideological rationalizations supplied by Secretary Acheson and may now sincerely believe that his "perpetual war for perpetual peace" program is a sound one and will ultimately bring peace and freedom to all mankind. There would seem to be some evidence to support this possibility in the long and elaborate "Profile" of President Truman by John Hersey in the *New Yorker* in 1951. Further confirmation may, perhaps, be found in the quasi-autobiographical portrayal of Mr. Truman, *Mr. President,* published in March 1952. This indicates that Mr. Truman's chief pride, relative to his seven years in the White House, is his imagined achievements in the cause of peace. At any rate it is certainly one of the most appalling proofs of the domination of doublethink over American public opinion today that the man whose policies, whatever their sources, have done more to spread the peace-by-war spirit over the globe than those of any other person in modern history can find it possible to regard himself as our greatest peace president and that millions of Americans can sincerely accept this fiction.

A related and almost equally impressive example of this doublethink is the alleged democratic basis of the global-meddling program. There are not more than one hundred thousand members of all world-government organizations combined, out of a total world population of nearly two and a half billion. This fact demonstrates that the global-meddling movement is, perhaps, the most extreme example of minority rule and influence in contemporary times, although it pretends to be battling for democracy beyond all else. In no totalitarian country of the twentieth century has so small a minority so completely controlled public policy. But, though a microscopic minority, numerically, the global-meddling groups enjoy almost a monopoly of the agencies of com-

---

[16]For a clear apprehension and exposition of the realities of the situation see the editorial, "America's Global New Deal," in *Truth*, June 1, 1951. See also Fred De Armond, "The One-World Illusion," *The Freeman*, April 7, 1952; Garet Garrett "Marks of Empire," *ibid.,* April 21, 1952; and, by the same author, *Rise of Empire* (Caldwell, Idaho: The Caxton Printers, Ltd., 1952).

munication and propaganda and public power vastly out of proportion to their numbers. In addition, they have the support of the greatest financial fortunes of our era. The Carnegie Foundation assists the movement because of its strong Anglophile tendency. The Rockefeller fortune is thrown behind it to facilitate political intervention in lands where it has vast oil interests. More recently, flying in the face of nearly everything that Henry Ford stood for in world affairs, the newly founded Ford Foundation has seemingly tried to outdo Carnegie and Rockefeller in promoting internationalism.

"Nineteen Eighty-Four" Trends Must Be Reversed

The urgent need for a reversal of the trend toward totalitarianism, military state capitalism, and "Nineteen Eighty-Four" patterns of life is obvious to discerning minds. But with this recognition comes the vital question of who will arise to expose the trends and induce us to retrace our steps before it is too late.

The Democrats surely will not, for they are the immediate beneficiaries of the trend. We may well recall here the observation of Robert R. Young that Democratic foreign policy since 1937 "has accomplished its objective, for it has kept in power (patronage and prominence), election after election, those who conceived and facilitated it." The late Arthur H. Vandenberg, Irving M. Ives, Wayne L. Morse, John Foster Dulles, Warren R. Austin, Harold E. Stassen, Thomas E. Dewey, Henry Cabot Lodge, Leverett Saltonstall, James H. Duff, and other "bipartisan" Republicans, have apparently made it impossible for the Republicans to check the trend to *Nineteen Eighty-Four*. Moreover, during the last five years, our economy has become so closely geared to vast armament and war expenditures that it is doubtful that any Republican president would dare to risk an abyssmal depression by seriously curtailing defense expenditures. An interventionist Republican, such as General Eisenhower, might even step up armament expenditures.

The business classes will not protest effectively because they enjoy the false prosperity engendered, with its lessening of competition, and have concentrated upon a campaign against a fictitious Santa Claus—attacking the bogus 3 percent welfare state as a leap into socialism and ignoring the fact that the cold, and ultimately hot, war is what is bringing on drastic and rigorous military state capitalism with all its elaborate state controls over industry and its ever-growing bureaucracy. Labor will not oppose the trend because it, also, is enjoying its "cut" in the temporary "gravy" produced by the cold war and the emergency armament program. The radicals are impotent, and most of the oldtime pacifists are either dead, or, like Edward Meade Earle, Paul H. Douglas, Reinhold Niebuhr, and others, have gone over ardently into the interventionist and cold-war camp.

There is little prospect that American intellectuals will take any stand against the trend toward a "Nineteen Eighty-Four" system. Most academicians are thoroughly indoctrinated with globaloney. The newspapers, on January 29, 1951, announced that some 875 leading historians and social scientists had heatedly approved the foreign policy of President Truman and Secretary Acheson, and denounced any return to neutrality and hemispheric defense, such as is suggested by ex-President Herbert Hoover. Even the scholars who recognize the dangers in current world trends are professionally intimidated and are afraid to speak out in support of their private convictions. As was indicated in the opening chapter of this book, the press, the radio, and television are overwhelmingly committed to the support of world-meddling and its inevitable reverberations on our domestic situation.

The recognition of the necessity for the reversal of current policy, if we are to have any hope of permanent peace and true prosperity, does not imply in the slightest a demand for any literal "isolationism." This is manifestly impossible in the type of world which has developed at the mid-century. Every country should collaborate to every reasonable extent in any promising international movement for peace. We should encourage the immediate establishment of limited and practical federations and work toward ultimate world government, however distant its actual realization may prove. But there can be no sound international policy in behalf of peace which deliberately splits the world into two or three hostile armed camps and takes pride in this achievement because of its temporary contribution to domestic political strategy, military prestige, full employment, and the postponement of depressions. The only sound foreign policy for the United States is a return to neutrality, which does not mean and never has meant any literal isolation. With this can be combined every possible effort to limit (not to extend) warfare, and to encourage better international understanding in every practical manner.

It is not necessary that a demand for the curtailing of the cold war carry with it any dangerous reduction of necessary defense measures. But the latter should be adjusted to the realization of the world situation and modern warfare techniques. They should not continue as a mere subordinate adjunct of domestic political and economic strategy.

There is surely no prospect of mitigating the cold war or reducing vast armament expenditures so long as every Russian proposal for peace, trade, or the adjustment of disputes is instantly rejected as a trick and smeared as a lie. Stalin's reputation for political veracity may justly be suspect, but from the record it is certainly as good as that of Roosevelt or Churchill. Indeed, it is very evident that Roosevelt and Hopkins deceived themselves in regard to Stalin's policies, despite expert warning, rather than being extensively or repeatedly deceived by explicit promises made by the Soviet chief. At least we could safely go as far as to put Russia on the spot each time she makes a peace proposal and compel her to demonstrate its authenticity and good faith, if there be any.

How to Defend Ourselves against Communism

Communism is, indeed, a menace to the American way of life, with respect both to its economic traditions and its heritage of freedom, however unlikely any military attack by the Soviet Union upon the United States may be, unless such an attack is provoked as a measure of preventive war. But, certainly, the best defense of the United States against Communism is a prosperous country in which the prosperity is real and enduring, is well distributed throughout the mass of the populace, and is founded upon the well-being of our own country rather than the political and economic bribery of foreign allies.

Equally valuable and potent as a defense against Communism is the assurance and perpetuation of our heritage of freedom and liberty, which no totalitarian country can provide, whatever material blessings it might ultimately confer upon its citizens. Just to the extent that the cold war gives birth to regimentation and witch-hunting in the United States, so far do we reduce our defenses against Communist propaganda and our superiority to the communistic way of life and daily make ourselves more like Soviet Russia.

The Soviet program for communizing the world is not based on a plan of military conquest. It is founded upon propaganda, infiltration, and intrigue. Such ideological revolutions have never yet been extinguished by military force. Not even Metternich was able to accomplish this. They must be met and overcome by a stronger and sounder ideology. American policy, if wisely conducted, could readily supply just this. But it will fail if our resources are squandered in lavish military outlays which cannot directly check ideological aggression, if our cold-war patterns increase regimentation and obliterate the libertarian superiorities which we enjoy over Soviet Russia and other totalitarian lands, and if astronomical military budgets undermine our economy and destroy any hope of sound and lasting prosperity. Without any major war on his hands, President Truman has levied more federal taxes than all the other American chief executives. During his administration, $264 billion in taxes have been accessed; all other presidents, from Washington to Truman, had levied only $248 billion. From the time of George Washington to that of Franklin D. Roosevelt, only $136 billion in taxes had been levied.

Several discerning writers have emphasized the fact that probably the most alarming aspect of our current agitation over Communism is that, in our effort to battle against it, we have succumbed to measures which daily make us more like the Soviets. There have been inroads on our liberty; witch-hunting has been on the increase. Elaborate state controls have been set up over industry, finance, living conditions, and personal behavior. There has been increasing militarization and the like. These things have brought about a marked similarity to "Nineteen Eighty-Four" conditions. In the society portrayed by George Orwell, the hated leader of the enemy, whose face is thrown on the screen to bring goose pimples and hisses during the daily hate periods, is Emmanuel Goldstein. But Goldstein is also the person who wrote the manual of political strategy and psychological warfare—the ideological "bible"—which is actually, if secretly, followed by the leaders in *Nineteen Eighty-Four*. There is grave danger that, in seeking to hold off Stalin, we shall take something more than a page out of his book.

The fallacy of imitating Russia in an effort to combat Soviet Communism has been well stated by F. A. Harper in his brochure *In Search of Peace;*

> Russia is supposed to be the enemy. Why? We are told that it is because Russia is communistic, and our enemy is communism.
>
> But if it is necessary for us to embrace extensive socialist-communist measures in order to fight a nation which has adopted them—"because *they* have adopted these measures"—why fight them? Why not join them in the first place and save all the bloodshed?
>
> ...There is no sense in our conjuring up in our minds a violent hatred against people who are the victims of communism in some foreign nation, when the same governmental shackles are making us servile to the illiberal forces at home.[17]

If the only methods available to exploit the great advantages and opportunities of our impressive technology, promote prosperity, and avert depressions were vast armament projects, there might be some excuse for linking our economy and life patterns to the cold-war program. But this is not the case in the slightest degree. In addition to the industry and employment which can be furnished by private enterprise, there are over four hundred billion dollars' worth of public works projects, many of them self-liquidating, which are sadly needed by the American public, and which would guarantee prosperity and freedom from depression for an indefinite period. Private enterprise could and should, of course, share widely and deeply in the execution of such projects.

In his address before the Michigan legislature on May 15, 1952, General Douglas MacArthur pointed out clearly our failure to provide for our own public needs while lavishing money on foreign boondoggling, even foreign "WPA" projects:

> We have but recently witnessed the stark reality of tragedy and distress brought to thousands of American homes over the area of eight states by the inundation of flood waters from the Missouri and Mississippi rivers. Such tragedy could and should have been avoided.
>
> I recall over forty years ago working as an engineer officer on plans for the control of just such flood conditions. Such plans have long been perfected and engineers, both military and civilian, time and time again have appealed for the funds needed for the control measures indicated. But such funds were never forthcom-

[17]Irvington-on-Hudson, N.Y.: The Foundation for Economic Education, 1951, pp. 35–37.

ing for so essential a protection of our own people, even though we remitted funds in far greater amounts to the peoples of Western Europe for purposes which included the consummation of similar protective projects. This is but one of the many cases wherein policy has furthered the interests of others at the expense of our own.

So far as any military effort can be used to undermine Communism, it must be limited mainly to letting the Communists fight among themselves. This can best be accomplished by ceasing to line up the rest of the world as a military threat to Communism. The latter policy only binds the Communists together. With this threat and pressure, there would soon appear many "Titoist" revolts, some of them, as in the case of China, of formidable proportions. It would have been very easy, beginning in 1947, to have encouraged Chinese patriotic sentiments and to have detached the Chinese Communists from Moscow. The Chinese Communists have a strong nationalist feeling and this could readily have been directed toward recovering the vast area of former Chinese territory now in the hands of Russia. Moreover, the United States can, far more effectively than Soviet Russia, supply the desperate need of Communist China for financial and technical aid. Our foreign policy since 1947, and especially since 1950, has only served to drive China into the arms of the Kremlin, no matter how reluctantly. It has also helped to align the great revolutionary trends in Asia and Africa with Russia, since the United States has assumed leadership of those forces which seek to maintain the *status quo* of colonialism and imperialism in the Old World. This is a matter of prime importance. The temporary superiority of the United States in technology and natural resources is not likely to counter successfully the vast Asiatic superiority in manpower and morale if all the revolutionary dynamics of Asia are also linked with Communist ideology and military strategy.

It is obvious, too, that in so fluid a situation as exists in the world today, no absolute or dogmatic predictions about the political and economic future can be plausible or command much respect. We may move rapidly from the cold war into a hot war and the destruction of civilization. Or, perhaps, the reluctance of the Western European nations to be extinguished, while serving as the cannon fodder and battlefields of a third world war, may check the war fever and compel political and economic leadership in both the United States and Russia to seek peace and to build a prosperous economy on the foundation of the well-being of the citizens rather than on phony war scares. The intensely hostile reaction of Europeans to the *Collier's* issue on the third world war indicated that these nations are less cordial to the actuality of such a war than they are to the financial handouts of the United States, ostensibly given to them to prepare for this very conflict.

The next decade or so will probably decide which line of development will be followed. At the present time we can do no more than to state with assurance that, unless the cold war is terminated and a third world war is prevented, there will be neither peace nor prosperity in the United States or elsewhere. Indeed, very little of what now passes for civilization could survive a third world conflict of the proportions which it would inevitably assume, fought with the unrestrained savagery and ruthlessness which the Nuremberg and Tokyo trials have assured and made inevitable. If the losers are bound to be tortured, humiliated, tried, and hanged, whatever their initial guilt, then nothing which might assure victory can be withheld, whatever its lethal destructiveness.

Postscript: An English View of *Nineteen Eighty-Four*

While preparing this chapter on the development of Orwellian society in the United States, I wrote to an eminent English publicist for his opinion of the validity of Orwell's pattern of prediction and received the following letter. It is printed here as a revealing appraisal of how an astute English thinker regards the thesis of the book and illustrates the Orwellian trends that he discerns in English political life at present.

I have now read and inwardly digested (so far as I can) *Nineteen Eighty-Four* by George Orwell.

It is certainly a brilliant piece of work. I think that it is a delightful touch that the central character is named Winston Smith: having been born around 1944, in common with many other infants at that time, he was named after the National Hero of that epoch!

On the whole, I cannot find a flaw in his arguments regarding the general lay-out of Power Politics in A.D. 1984. It is all too likely that, by that time, the Soviets will have overrun the entire

Continent of Europe, leaving only Britain as an "Atlantic Island" dependency of the U.S.A. China, too, will probably have asserted her national independence of Moscow, being too vast a country to come entirely within the Soviet orbit, and there being no "natural" frontier in Central Asia between the Chinese and Russian Empires.

At present it seems rather doubtful whether the Soviets would ever be in a position to contest the possession of North Africa with "Oceania"; but, of course, with the absorption of Western Europe, including Germany, France and Spain, the Soviet war potential would be enormously increased, as the resources of the Ruhr-Lorraine-Saar-Luxemburg area would be at their disposal.

One can almost see even today the beginnings of the process which Orwell describes so graphically. Clearly Churchill is carefully keeping clear of European commitments, so as to be able to evacuate Europe at short notice. There is, too, a suggestion of "Ingsoc" in Churchill's peremptory dismissal of Parliament until ordered to reassemble to hear and approve what has been decided at Washington.

The whole technique of Government seems to be changing. The Press positively exudes pessimism: the *Evening News* tells us in glaring headlines that "this is going to be the Worst Year since 1945"! All the stress is laid on "sacrifices" in the cause of "defence": there is no longer the suggestion of "a better time round the corner." Disarmament (which used to be the keynote in every discussion between the Wars) is now hardly ever mentioned. Very occasionally a "disarmament plan" is put forward in U.N.O., but only with the obvious intention of putting the "enemy" in the wrong, by including conditions which he will never accept!

It seems to be tacitly agreed that the "cold war" is to last indefinitely, as a means of fomenting hatred of the "enemy," but it must not be allowed to turn into "hot war"—at least, not yet. That was apparently why MacArthur fell from favour; he wanted a full-dress war against China; whereas Truman and his advisers preferred to limit the actual fighting zone to Korea. But neither side really wants to end the Korean war—the Armistice negotiations are perpetually "breaking down" over some triviality.

The accent is on "Austerity": most of the available raw materials must go to swell the "export drive" or into munitions. There is to be a chronic "shortage" of everything. At the Election, the Tories were very careful not to promise any concrete improvement. And now that they are themselves in power, they probably don't find "State Ownership" as onerous as they did before, because "State Ownership" in practice means "Ruling Party Ownership" and they are the Party in power.

George Orwell is right when he says that every revolution in history—e.g. The French Revolution—was made, not by the lower classes, but by the middle classes, who used the masses as tools to lever the upper classes out of power and themselves into power. He may be right when he asserts that the device of transferring theoretically all property to the "State" will give to the ruling class absolute power, while the "proles" will be kept in subjection by maintaining a perpetual state of "cold war" and ascribing all their hardships to the "enemy."

But, of course, we have not yet reached that happy state. The workers may react violently when the full results of Churchill's mission reveal themselves. I think it is highly significant that the Home Guard is being re-organised: it is not invasion, but civil disorder that has to be guarded against! Nevertheless, the process of regimentation has made great progress; Conscription, for example, is now accepted as a part of our daily life.

To sum up: I think that Orwell's main contention that "cold war" is now an essential feature of normal life is being verified more and more from day to day. No one now really believes in a "peace settlement" with the Soviets, and many people in positions of power regard such a prospect with positive horror. A war footing is the only basis of full employment. Between big Power blocs there is no question of "fighting for markets." The *Daily Mail* is trying to revive the bogy of German competition, but that is an out-of-date conception. So long as Britain is tied to American capitalism, and so long as American capitalism continues to function, we must resign ourselves to seeing our country used merely as a cog in a big machine.

RECOMMENDED READING

Alperovitz, Gar. *Cold War Essays.* Cambridge, Mass.: Schenkman, 1970.

Ambrose, Stephen E. *Rise to Globalism: American Foreign Policy, 1938-1976.* New York: Penguin, 1976.

Aspin, Les. "How to Look at the Soviet-American Balance." *Foreign Policy* 22 (Spring 1976): 96-106.

Barnes, Harry Elmer. "A. J. P. Taylor and the Causes of World War II." *New Individualist Review* 2 (Spring 1962): 3-16.

———. *Perpetual War for Perpetual Peace.* Caldwell, Idaho: Caxton, 1953.

Barnet, Richard. "Promise of Disarmament." *New York Times Magazine,* 27 February 1977, p. 16.

———. *Roots of War.* New York: Penguin, 1973.

Beard, Charles A. *President Roosevelt and the Coming of the War, 1941.* New Haven: Yale University Press, 1948.

Chamberlin, William H. *America's Second Crusade.* Colorado Springs, Colo.: Ralph Myles, 1962.

Doenecke, Justus D. *The Literature of Isolationism: A Guide to Non-interventionist Scholarship, 1930-1972.* Colorado Springs, Colo.: Ralph Myles, 1972.

Ekirch, Arthur A., Jr. *The Decline of American Liberalism.* New York: Atheneum, 1969.

———. *The Civilian and the Military: A History of the American Anti-military Tradition.* Colorado Springs, Colo.: Ralph Myles, 1972.

Fleming, D. F. *The Cold War and Its Origins, 1917-1960.* New York: Doubleday, 1961.

Flynn, John T. *As We Go Marching.* New York: Free Life, 1973.

Gaddis, John L. *The United States and the Origins of the Cold War, 1941-1947.* New York: Columbia University Press, 1972.

Gardner, Lloyd C. *Architects of Illusion: Men and Ideas in American Foreign Policy, 1941–1949.* New York: Watts, 1972.

Garrett, Garet. "Rise of Empire." In *The People's Pottage.* Caldwell, Idaho: Caxton, 1953.

Goddard, Arthur, ed. *Harry Elmer Barnes, Learned Crusader: The New History in Action.* Colorado Springs: Ralph Myles, 1968.

Kolko, Gabriel. *The Politics of War: The World and United States Foreign Policy, 1943–1945.* New York: Random House, 1968.

LaFeber, Walter. *America, Russia and the Cold War, 1945#1975.* New York: Wiley, 1976.

——, ed. *America in the Cold War: Twenty Years of Revolution and Response, 1947–1967.* New York: Wiley, 1969.

Lens, Sidney. *The Futile Crusade: Anti-Communism as American Credo.* Chicago: Quadrangle, 1964.

Liggio, Leonard P. *Why the Futile Crusade?* New York: Center for Libertarian Studies, 1978.

——, and Martin, James J., eds. *Watershed of Empire: Essays on New Deal Foreign Policy.* Colorado Springs, Colo.: Ralph Myles, 1976.

Martin, James J. *American Liberalism and World Politics.* Old Greenwich, Conn.: Devin-Adair, 1963.

——. *Revisionist Viewpoints: Essays in a Dissident Historical Tradition.* Colorado Springs, Colo.: Ralph Myles, 1971.

Melman, Seymour. *Pentagon Capitalism: The Political Economy of War.* New York: McGraw-Hill, 1970.

Mises, Ludwig von. *Liberalism: A Socioeconomic Exposition.* Kansas City: Sheed Andrews & McMeel, 1978.

Morley, Felix. *The Foreign Policy of the United States.* New York: Knopf, 1951.

Radosh, Ronald. *Prophets on the Right: Conservative Critics of American Globalism.* New York: Simon & Schuster, 1975.

Ravenal, Earl C. *Never Again: Learning from America's Foreign Policy Failures.* Philadelphia: Temple University Press, 1978.

Russett, Bruce M. *No Clear and Present Danger: A Skeptical View of the United States Entry into World War II.* New York: Harper & Row, 1972.

Stone, I. F. *The Hidden History of the Korean War.* New York: Monthly Review, rev. ed. 1969.

Sumner, William Graham. *The Conquest of the United States by Spain, and Other Essays.* Chicago: Regnery, 1965.

Taft, Robert. *A Foreign Policy for Americans.* Garden City, N.Y.: Doubleday, 1951.

Tansill, Charles C. *America Goes to War* (1938). Reprint. Gloucester, Mass.: Peter Smith, 1963.

———. *Back Door to War: The Roosevelt Foreign Policy, 1933–1941.* Chicago: Regnery, 1952.

Veale, F. J. P. *Advance to Barbarism: A Reexamination.* Old Greenwich, Conn.: Devin-Adair, 1968.

Williams, William A. *The Tragedy of American Diplomacy.* New York: Dell, 1972.

ABOUT THE AUTHOR

Harry Elmer Barnes (1889-1968), American historian and sociologist, was one of the principal exponents of twentieth-century revisionism. Born in Auburn, New York, he received his Ph.D. from Columbia in 1918. He taught at Syracuse, Amherst, Columbia, Smith, Temple, Barnard, Clark, the University of Colorado, Washington State University, Indiana State University, and the New School for Social Research.

Barnes wrote in many disciplines with remarkable assurance and intuition. The *New Columbia Encyclopedia* (1975) says that "his ability to synthesize information from various fields into an intelligible pattern showing human development profoundly affected the teaching of history." Commenting on Barnes's work on World War I, George Peabody Gooch noted: "No other American scholar has done so much to familiarize his countrymen with the new evidence and to compel them to revise their wartime judgments in the light of this new material."

Among his books are *Social History of the Western World* (1921), *History and Social Intelligence* (1926), *The History of Western Civilization* (2 vols., 1935), *An Intellectual and Cultural History of the Western World* (3 vols., 1937), *Perpetual War for Perpetual Peace* (1953), and *Social Thought from Lore to Science* (1961).

The Cato Papers

Reprinted by the Cato Institute, the Papers in this series have been selected for their singular contributions to such fields as economics, history, philosophy, and public policy.

Copies of the *Cato Papers* may be ordered from the Publications Department, Cato Institute, 747 Front Street, San Francisco, California 94111.